USS Arizona

Written by David Doyle

Squadron At Sea®

Cover Art by Don Greer

Squadron Signal® Publications

Line Illustrations by Todd Sturgell

(Front Cover) USS *Arizona* steams idyllically off the Hawaiian coast in August 1941, just four months before her date with destiny. Her mundane Measure 1 camouflage scheme, broken by the red tops of her forward turrets, indicates her Battleship Division One assignment, and the red top of turret four identifies her specifically to her spotter plane pilots.

(Back Cover) Prior to her 1929 modernization, *Arizona's* masts resembled cages, as in this rendering of her riding at anchor in 1918, with a 48-star flag fluttering in the sea breeze at her stern.

About the Squadron® At Sea Series

The *Squadron At Sea* series details a specific ship using color and black-and-white archival photographs and photographs of in-service, preserved, and restored equipment. *Squadron At Sea* titles are devoted to civilian and military vessels, while *On Deck®* titles are devoted to warships. These picture books focus on specific vessels from the laying of the keel to present or its finale.

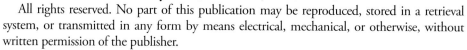

Proudly printed in the U.S.A.
Copyright 2015, 2011 Squadron/Signal Publications
1115 Crowley Drive, Carrollton, TX 75006-1312 U.S.A.

Hard Cover ISBN 978-0-89747-641-6
Soft Cover ISBN 978-0-89747-640-9

Military/Combat Photographs and Snapshots

If you have any photos of aircraft, armor, soldiers, or ships of any nation, particularly wartime snapshots, please share them with us and help make Squadron/Signal's books all the more interesting and complete in the future. Any photograph sent to us will be copied and returned. Electronic images are preferred. The donor will be fully credited for any photos used. Please send them to:

Squadron/Signal Publications
1115 Crowley Drive
Carrollton, TX 75006-1312 U.S.A.
www.SquadronSignalPublications.com

(Title Page) The USS *Arizona* (BB-39) heads out to sea following her modernization in the early 1930s. *Arizona* was designed in 1912 specifically to fight in a war with Japan in the Pacific Ocean: a war that would not come until almost 30 years after the ship was conceived. The *Arizona* had never fired its big guns in combat when it was sunk at Pearl Harbor by the Japanese on 7 December 1941. To this day, the remains of the *Arizona* lie on the bottom of the harbor as a memorial to the 1,177 men killed on her. (National Archives)

Dedication

To the men and women who forged *Arizona* and walked her decks in peacetime, and to the men who sleep with her today.

Introduction

Visitors flock to the USS *Arizona* memorial, gazing silently, some speaking in hushed tones, often weeping, as they stare at the ghostly apparition that is the hulk of the *Arizona's* hull resting beneath the oil-stained waters of Pearl Harbor. Few can visualize her imposing stature on the evening of 6 December 1941 – her masts towering 125 feet above the water's surface and teakwood decks, polished until almost white, abuzz with the bustle of her 1,511-man crew, some going about their routine, others preparing to go ashore for weekend liberty. Her fuel tanks had been topped off and held 1.5 million gallons of thick Bunker-C oil in anticipation for Monday morning's departure for the U.S. West Coast. Today, her hull rests on the harbor floor, an occasional drop of oil rising to the surface, said to be the tears of *Arizona* herself weeping for her lost crew, over a thousand of whom remain entombed in her.

Arizona today is remembered, deservedly so, as a memorial to the 1,177 men killed aboard her on 7 December 1941 (some are interred at the National Memorial Cemetery of the Pacific – the "Punchbowl") and the attack that propelled the United States into World War II. But before that single day of infamy, *Arizona* had been a valuable member of the U.S. fleet for 9,182 days, and that after 946 days of construction. No doubt because of the horror and gravity of 7 December 1941, all the preceding days are virtually forgotten. In the mourning for the 1,177 lost, the legions that walked her decks before them are often forgotten.

Through the hundreds of engineers and draftsman who designed her, to the tens of thousands of shipyard workers had swarmed over her on the East and West coasts, building and maintaining her, to thousands of crewmen who came and went, the countless visitors she welcomed, and even during a turn at being a Hollywood starlet, *Arizona* was once very much alive, animated by the lives of countless men and women who touched her.

Acknowledgments

The preparation of this book was a substantial undertaking, and the completion of this project required the help of many individuals, some of whom have devoted years to researching the *Arizona*. Their unselfish help is deeply appreciated In particular I would like to thank Tom Kailbourn; Tracy White (Researcher at Large); Ron Smith; Scott Taylor; Robert Hanshew with the Navy History and Heritage Command; Don Preul; Daniel Martinez, Amanda Corona, and Scott Pawlowski at the WWII Valor in the Pacific National Monument; Marcus Robbins; Cristy Gallardo with the U.S. Navy; the Puget Sound Maritime Historical Society; Judith Bowman at the U.S. Army Museum of Hawaii; Michael W. Pocock and www.maritimequest.com; Claudia Jew and Thomas Moore at the Mariners' Museum; the Sharlot Hall Museum, the Franklin D. Roosevelt Presidential Library; National Park Service Submerged Resources Center; the staffs of the National Archives, the *Arizona* State Archives, and the Hawaii State Archives and the Library of Congress. The dedicated and talented staff at Squadron Publications capably assembled this volume, and painstakingly restored aging, damaged photos. My darling wife Denise scanned the vast majority of the photos shown on these pages, in addition to providing unflagging encouragement and support during long hours of research.

Britain's HMS *Dreadnought* ushered in a whole new age of battleship design in 1906, establishing the basic pattern that the USS *Arizona* would follow. (Naval History and Heritage Command)

Birth of a Legend

During the early years of the 20th century, battleships were not only the embodiment of sea power, they were also tangible evidence of a *nation's* power. All warships are complex, expensive pieces of machinery, none was more so during that time than a battleship. Battleships were the Edwardian symbol of a superpower – lesser nations simply could not afford the huge cost of building and operating such vessels, particularly after the advent of the revolutionary HMS *Dreadnought,* launched February 1906.

Prior to *Dreadnought,* capital ships were armed with an array of weapons of varying caliber, with the general theory of using a comparable size weapon to engage various types of enemy vessels. That is, for example, a five-inch gun would fire on destroyers, an eight-inch on cruisers, and a 12-inch on battleships. *Dreadnought* changed that, with only two broad types of weapons, small guns for defense against torpedo boats, and all-big guns of the same caliber as her offensive armament. Regardless of nation, battleships constructed in this style became known as dreadnoughts.

Within five years of her launch, HMS *Dreadnought* had been eclipsed by a new type of ship, dubbed the super-dreadnought. The distinction is based upon a significant increase in displacement (25 percent) and an increase in the size and number of main guns, such that the weight of the shells fired in a single broadside was double that of the *Dreadnought.* For the United States Navy, the *New York* class (USS *New York* and USS *Texas*), laid down in 1911 and each displacing 27,000 tons and armed with 10 14-inch rifles, marked the beginning of the super-dreadnought era. The weakness of the *New Yorks* and other early super-dreadnoughts was their vulnerability to the plunging shell-fall commensurate with the ever-increasing range capabilities of heavy naval guns. The follow-on *Nevada*-class ships would address this deficiency, and many others.

3

The USS *Nevada* (BB-36), seen here, and her sister ship, USS *Oklahoma* (BB-37), were the precursors of the USS *Arizona* and her sister ship, USS *Pennsylvania* (BB-38). All four ships were similar in concept, but *Nevada* and *Oklahoma* were lighter in weight, shorter in length, and with a smaller main battery: 10 14-inch guns instead of the *Arizona*'s and *Pennsylvania*'s 12 14-inch guns. (National Archives)

USS *Pennsylvania*, sister ship of the *Arizona*, rests at anchor before its 1929-1931 modernization. Though these two vessels were very similar in appearance, *Pennsylvania*'s bridge was higher than *Arizona*'s. *Pennsylvania* survived the Pearl Harbor attack, served in World War II, and was a target ship in the 1946 Bikini Atoll atomic tests. She was finally sunk as a target for conventional weapons in 1948. (National Archives)

As battleship armament became more powerful, naval architects sought to increase the armor protection of their ships. The standard for the United States Navy was that a battleship should be able to withstand shellfire from its twin. Naturally enough this led to ever-increasing weights, and often decreases in speed and range. Higher speed meant more powerful, and often bulkier engines, which in turn meant hulls of greater volume. That led to more surface area to protect, and a vicious cycle of ship design ensued.

With the *Nevada*-class, a new armor theory came to the forefront. Rather than trying to provide some degree of protection to the entire ship, the *Nevada*-class introduced the all-or-nothing armor arrangement. The critical portions of the ship, navigation, propulsion, and armament were well-armored; non-critical areas such as berthing, fuel and water storage were provided with almost no protection. This allowed the same tonnage of armor to better protect the ship's essential features more thoroughly than had previously been possible. The all-or-nothing principle was carried forward into the *Pennsylvania*-class, of which *Arizona* was a member, as well as all subsequent U.S. battleships.

Not surprisingly, especially considering the great expense involved, (the *Arizona* cost almost $13 million in 1914, a year when the average U.S. autoworker made $2.34 a day), design and construction of new battleships was fraught with a great deal of politics, both nationally, and among the various agencies within the Navy. The paperwork, both in terms of design as well as the red tape, could take years to complete. No sooner than the design work for the *Nevadas* had been completed in 1911 did the U.S. Navy General Board turn its attention to "battleship 1913," the follow-on design, which would include *Arizona*. The Bureau of Construction and Repair favored building more vessels of the established *Nevada* design, but the General Board sought greater firepower and increased protection from torpedos.

The "Battleship 1911" design had incorporated 10 14-inch guns spread among four turrets, two triples and two twins. In keeping with the General Board's desires, however, the proposed "Battleship 1913" would be armed with 12 guns of the same type, housed in four triple turrets. The new ships would additionally feature a 3-inch thick torpedo bulkhead made of Special Treated Steel (STS) spaced 9-feet 6-inches from the ships' outer bottoms, with the void between forming a sort of cushion against torpedo explosions.

The General Board asked Congress to fund four of the new ships in 1913, and Congress responded with approval and funding for one. "Battleship 1913" became "Battleship 38" when authorized by 22 August 1912. Named *Pennsylvania,* following a lengthy bidding process, the new ship was ordered from Newport News Shipbuilding and Drydock Company, with delivery set for three years in the future. It was specified that *Pennsylvania* was to be equipped as a fleet flagship, with accommodations for an Admiral and his staff, in addition to that of the ship's own captain.

The next year the General Board, as had become routine, debated many changes and improvements in battleship design before ultimately compromising with an agreement that the proposed "Battleship 1914" design would be a duplicate of "Battleship 1913." Once again the General Board recommended, and the Secretary of the Navy requested of Congress, authorization and funding to build multiple ships, this time three. Yet again, Congress granted funding for only one. Duplicating *Pennsylvania*, albeit with a smaller conning tower and flat armor of the uptakes, eliminated considerable design time. To further speed delivery, "Battleship 39" was ordered from the New York Navy Yard, circumventing the time-consuming bid process. A delivery date of September 1916 was specified. Battleship 39 would go down in history as **Arizona.**

A group of VIPs walk down the hull plates of Battleship 39 at the keel-laying ceremony on 16 March 1914. The two men leading the procession are Assistant Secretary of the Navy (and future President) Franklin D. Roosevelt (left) and Captain Albert Gleaves, commandant of the New York Navy Yard. In the background are some of the navy yard buildings. (Naval History and Heritage Command)

At the laying of the keel at the New York Navy Yard on chilly, hazy 16 March 1914, a crane lowers the ceremonial first keel plate onto the building ways. Actually, for months prior to the ceremony, workers at the yard had been laying out hull plates and structural parts on the ways, ready to be adjusted in place and riveted following the keel laying. (Franklin D. Roosevelt Library)

The little boy hanging onto Franklin D. Roosevelt's finger is three-year-old Henry Williams Jr., a naval contractor's son, who had the honor of inserting the first ceremonial bolt in the keel. Williams would grow up to become a naval officer, and, as a lieutenant, he would watch the *Arizona* as it burned on the evening of 7 December 1941. (Franklin D. Roosevelt Library)

An article headlined "Biggest Warship in the World Begun Here" appeared on page 16 of the *New York Tribune* on 17 March 1914. It carried a report about the previous day's keel-laying for "Battleship 39," claiming that "the new vessel is to be named the *North Carolina*." U.S. Navy ship names are assigned by the Secretary of the Navy, sometimes bowing to political pressure. The Secretary of the Navy at the time of *Arizona's* construction, Josephus Daniels, tended to name battleships for states that had voted solidly for the president who appointed him – Woodrow Wilson. Daniels himself hailed from North Carolina, which no doubt is the origin of the published speculation regarding the name of "Battleship 39." The official name *Arizona* would not be determined until later in construction. While *Arizona* retained her hull number "39" throughout her life, on 17 July 1920 the U.S. Navy changed the official ship numbering system, and "Battleship 39" became "BB-39." (Library of Congress)

5

The keel-laying ceremony for Battleship 39 on 16 March 1914 is viewed from a distance, facing forward. Many of the plates that would form the outer skin of the hull are lying on the wooden supporting frame, waiting to be fastened together. Materials for the ship began arriving at the New York Navy Yard, in Brooklyn, on 3 November 1913. (National Archives)

By 3 May 1914, the frame of *Arizona* was taking shape. As seen from the forward starboard beam, many of the vertical frames are in place, and the torpedo bulkheads erected on each side of the frame are partially completed. The inboard bulkhead was of 60-pound treated steel plate, while the outboard bulkhead was normal structural steel plate. (National Archives)

Some transverse bulkheads for the machinery spaces were in place by 2 June 1914 in this view from the stern. The manner in which the outer plates of the hull were laid down and then the frame members were attached to them is apparent. Several plates that have been fastened to each other but are yet to be secured to the frame are in the foreground. (National Archives)

On the same date, the fireroom (foreground) was photographed from the port side. A dozen Babcock & Wilcox boilers would be installed here; the uptake, or funnel, would be built above them. Compressed-air hoses for the rivet guns are draped over the bulkheads and frames. The tops of the ship's frames were angled to conform to the angled outer part of the splinter deck that would be installed later. (National Archives)

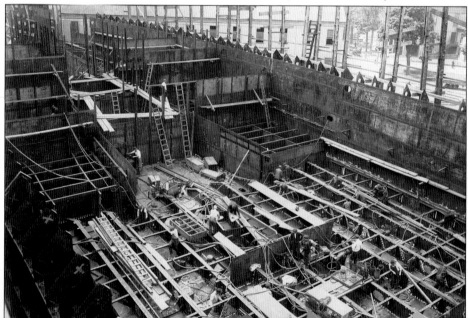

When compared to the photo taken from the same location from the stern on 2 June, this view taken on 2 July 1914 shows the progress that was made in one month. Framing to support a platform deck is taking shape, and frame 122 is present in the foreground. Later the barbettes of turrets three and four would be constructed in the center of this area. (National Archives)

This view towards the stern from 14 September 1914 shows the framing that will support the third, or splinter, deck is taking shape. This deck, which would have 1.5-inch STS (special treatment steel) on the sloping sides and 1-inch STS on the main surface, was intended to limit the damage from any projectiles that pierced the belt armor or the armored second deck. (National Archives)

This view taken on 2 July 1914 from the outboard side of the port torpedo bulkhead of the ship facing aft shows the tops of the frames, which were spaced four feet apart. The tops of the frames were angled to support the outer part of the splinter deck, a sloping structure of 1.5-inch armor plate that would cover the space to the right of the photo. In service, oil would be stored in that space and would provide buffering against torpedoes. (National Archives)

7

It is now 16 September 1914 and plates are being laid down for the third deck. Like the frame members to which they were attached, the deck plates were predrilled to accept fasteners. Such predrilling required precise planning and layout to ensure that everything fit correctly. This view is from the port beam facing toward the bow. (National Archives)

Work is progressing on the second deck, as viewed from the port side looking aft on 4 March 1915. To the left is the barbette of turret one, with the barbettes for turrets two through four visible aft of it. At this point, most of the visible plates for the deck and barbettes were tacked in place with nuts and bolts, with riveting to follow. (National Archives)

On 6 October 1914, a wooden derrick erected on deck is hoisting plate armor for installation on deck. The plate has identifying markings on it, including the number 96570. The second deck, designated the armored deck, was laminated with two layers of 50# STS and one layer of 20# MS (mild steel), for a total thickness of 3 inches. (National Archives)

The second deck as it appeared on 4 March 1915 is viewed from the turret-two barbette, with the turret-three barbette rising in the distance. The large opening in the deck in the foreground was for the uptake. On the vertical plates to the left, the frame numbers are marked in white. Numbers 71 and 72 are faintly visible to the extreme left. (National Archives)

Also photographed on 4 March 1915 was this view forward from the turret-one barbette. The second deck has been assembled, and in the distance, work has started on the main deck and the bow. When completed, the barbettes would have up to 13 inches of armor and would contain the machinery and ammunition-handling spaces for the turrets. (National Archives)

This magnificent panoramic photograph of *Arizona* was taken on 18 June 1915, the day before her launching. Her sides were completed up to the gunwales of the main deck (left half of the photo) and the forecastle deck (right half of the photo). The superstructure, masts, turrets, belt armor, and other components would be installed after the launching. Noteworthy features in the photo include the bilge keel forward of the outboard propeller shaft; the round opening above the forward end of the bilge keel for the main condenser intake, aft starboard torpedo tube above the outboard prop shaft (both aft tubes were eliminated before the ship went into service); and the two casemates near the stern and eight casemates below the forecastle deck for the 5-inch/51-caliber guns of the secondary battery. The screws, or propellers, would be installed after launching. (Stan Piet collection)

9

The forecastle deck is seen from the bow of *Arizona* the day before her launch. Much work remains to be done on the superstructure and the barbettes, but the conning tower, surrounded by scaffolding, is beginning to take shape. In the distance are two massive, movable cranes that were essential to the ship's construction. (National Archives)

At the stern of *Arizona* was a single, massive balanced rudder, each side exposing 443 square feet of area to guide the ship. Normally, the rudder was controlled electrically in response to helm inputs from the bridge. *Arizona* also had a backup system that utilized steam-driven pistons to turn the rudder. Also present was a manual third system, called the auxiliary steering, whereby teams of sailors deep in the ship turned huge ship's wheels and manually moved the rudder. (The Mariners' Museum)

The aft end of the port cradle that, along with the starboard cradle, supported *Arizona* during construction is displayed on the day of the ship's launching. The second from aft port casemate is also in view, as well as the round opening for the aft port side torpedo tube, forward of the outboard propeller shaft, and, to the far left, the port bilge keel. (National Archives)

Similar features are shown on the starboard side of the stern on the day of launching. This part of the launching cradle was also known as the stern poppet. There were also port and starboard fore poppets, all of which worked to distribute the ship's weight on the launching ways. Poppets were constructed of wood and fit very snugly to the hull. (National Archives)

10

Old Glory waves briskly from *Arizona's* flag staff as workmen stand by next to the port stern poppet on the day of the launch. To prepare the ship for launching, workmen spent hours that day methodically knocking out the supports that the ship was built on, transferring its stupendous weight to the ways on which she would slide into the water. (National Archives)

It was estimated that over fifty thousand spectators witnessed the launching of *Arizona* under a clear, blue sky on Saturday, 19 June 1915. Patriotic bunting decorated the forecastle and the stand to the lower left, where the ship's sponsor, Miss Esther Ross, a 17-year-old resident of Prescott, Arizona, and her entourage have just arrived. (National Archives)

Members of the State of Arizona's delegation to the launching of *Arizona* included, left to right, Miss Eva Behn, Mrs. W. W. Ross (mother of the ship's sponsor, Miss Esther Ross), Secretary of the Navy Josephus Daniels, Arizona Governor George W. P. Hunt, and Esther Ross, who is holding the ceremonial christening bottles attached to a line. (University of Arizona Library)

Miss Esther Ross, the sponsor of *Arizona,* was the daughter of Prescott, Arizona, pioneer and pharmacist William W. Ross, who successfully lobbied state politicians to name Esther the sponsor of the new battleship. Before christening day, she practiced this ancient ritual at home by throwing water-filled bottles against a fence post. (Library of Congress)

Since Arizona was a dry state in 1915, it was decided to christen the ship with a bottle each of water as well as the traditional christening material, champagne. The christening bottles, fashioned by Tiffanys, held water from the Roosevelt Dam in Arizona and champagne from the M. Hommel Wine Company of Sandusky, Ohio. (Sharlot Hall Museum)

At 1:05 p.m. on 19 June 1915, workmen cut the last blocks holding the ship in place on the ways. Six cables attached to lugs on the sides of the bow, three per side, held the hull steady until launching. Visible on the hull below the waterline, adjacent to the building to the left, is the opening for the starboard torpedo tube. (Library of Congress)

After the cables holding the hull stationary were released, hydraulic levers were activated to start the hull moving. At 1:10 the *Arizona* began her short journey down the ways, at which moment Miss Ross christened the ship. In this photograph, the *Arizona* has neared the end of the ways as the crowd cheers her on. (National Archives)

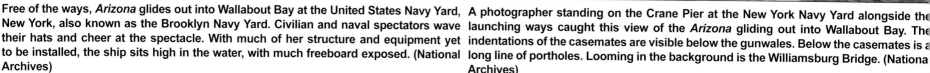

Free of the ways, *Arizona* glides out into Wallabout Bay at the United States Navy Yard, New York, also known as the Brooklyn Navy Yard. Civilian and naval spectators wave their hats and cheer at the spectacle. With much of her structure and equipment yet to be installed, the ship sits high in the water, with much freeboard exposed. (National Archives)

A photographer standing on the Crane Pier at the New York Navy Yard alongside the launching ways caught this view of the *Arizona* gliding out into Wallabout Bay. The indentations of the casemates are visible below the gunwales. Below the casemates is a long line of portholes. Looming in the background is the Williamsburg Bridge. (National Archives)

Another photograph taken from the end of the Crane Pier at the New York Navy Yard shows the *Arizona* moving farther out into the bay, with the East River in the background. Rising above the deck is the lower part of the conning tower. Numerous tugboats are getting into position to secure themselves to the otherwise powerless ship. (National Archives)

Tugboats move *Arizona* past pilings to her berth at Pier D on launching day. The bunting is still flapping from her forecastle. Moored to that pier, the ship would undergo the final phases of her fitting-out, which would last the next 16 months. In the background are the cage masts of various warships at the navy yard, including, beyond the bow of the *Arizona*, those of USS *Arkansas* (BB-33). (National Archives)

On launching day, lingering spectators look on as tug boats begin to move the *Arizona* to Pier D at New York Navy Yard, where construction on the ship will continue. On a wooden platform at the end of the Crane Pier to the right, a cameraman, very likely the same one who took the three preceding images, is taking photographs. (National Archives)

Among the components fitted to the USS *Arizona* after her launching were her guns. At the Naval Gun Factory, Washington, D.C., Navy Yard, 14-inch guns and smaller pieces such as those destined for the *Arizona* are under construction. When USS *Arizona* was built, most of the U.S. Navy's large-caliber guns were made at the Naval Gun Factory, although some large-caliber naval guns were also produced by Bethlehem Steel, Midvale Steel, and the Watervliet Arsenal. (Library of Congress)

The breech of a 14-inch gun is being bored while an inspector closely watches the operation with the aid of an electric light. During boring, the bit was frequently withdrawn to allow inspection, to ensure that the cut was true. Four cuts, two rough ones and two fine ones, were usually required to finish a bore. (Library of Congress)

The *Arizona's* 14-inch guns were of "built-up" construction: a laborious process whereby a central "tube" was forged, bored, lathed, and finished to very strict tolerances, and successive "hoops" were similarly machined and shrink-fitted over the tube. Subsequently, the assembled gun was milled on a massive lathe, rifled, fitted with a breech mechanism, and repeatedly inspected for flaws, warping, and distortion. Here, a bit is being positioned to bore the breech of a 14-inch gun at the Naval Gun Factory. (Library of Congress)

A 14-inch gun barrel under construction at the Naval Gun Factory is positioned in the shrinking pit, a square-sectioned well with room enough for workmen to operate in it. The building of the gun began by placing its liner in this pit, perfectly vertical. Then, the tube was heated in a hot-air furnace and carefully lowered over the liner, taking care not to let it prematurely stick to the liner. Cooling water was then employed to gradually shrink the tube in place. Then, more layers, called hoops, were added in the same manner. (Library of Congress)

A 14-inch/45-caliber gun barrel marked #188 is being lowered into the shrinking pit, breech end down, by means of an overhead crane. The Naval Gun Factory's shrinking pit was brick lined and had several work platforms in it. The barrel was placed in the shrinking pit either breech-end up or down, depending on whether hoops were being added toward the breech end or the muzzle end. The hoops added at the muzzle end served to form the "chase," the slight swelling of the barrel at the muzzle. (Library of Congress)

A sleeve of a 14-inch gun was photographed in a gun factory. It was bored to accommodate the barrel of the gun toward the breech end, and it was by means of the sleeve that the gun was installed on its recoil mount in the turret. Three sleeves were joined side by side to form the slide assembly, whereby all three guns elevated in unison. (Library of Congress)

In a view of the interior of a shop at the Naval Gun Factory, resting on a stand in the right background is a 14-inch gun barrel that appears to be in a fairly advanced state of construction, while smaller-gauge guns are arrayed in the foreground. To the left are belts, connected to powered shafts, which provided power to the milling machinery. (Library of Congress)

To the left, inspectors are using a star gauge, three rods set at 120-degree angles from each other and mounted on a long staff, to accurately measure the diameter of the bore of a 14-inch gun. A man at a table records data. To the right of that gun, another 14-inch gun is spinning on a lathe, undergoing a cutting operation on the outside of the barrel. (Library of Congress)

Two completed 14-inch guns are ready for shipment. Following testing at the Naval Proving Ground, they were returned to the gun factory for final inspection before being issued for service. Markings on the wooden plug affixed to the barrel on the left includes the number 154, stenciled weight data, and "Supply Officer / Navy Yard / Washington, D.C." (Library of Congress)

While a ship first takes to the sea at her launching, a warship begins her military career on the day of her commissioning. Upon commissioning, the custody of the ship transfers from the builder, whether commercial or military, to the active Navy, specifically her captain and crew. The pomp attendant upon the christening of a United States warship has grown through time, and had become fairly significant by 17 October 1916, the day when *Arizona* was placed in commission and the "U.S.S.," for United States Ship, became an official part of her identification. When she was photographed that day at the New York Navy Yard, *Arizona* was essentially complete, with her belt armor installed and cage masts, gun houses, conning tower, and other structures finished. (Library of Congress)

One day after her commissioning, *Arizona* is viewed from the aft part of the main deck facing forward, showing several open hatches. Turret four is turned to port, displaying one of the 14-inch/45-caliber guns in profile, including the muzzle chase and barrel step. Tampions, in effect large plugs, were fitted in the muzzles of the 14-inch guns to protect their bores from corrosion and foreign objects. (Library of Congress)

Rising above USS *Arizona's* aft 14-inch turrets is the main mast. Partway up the mast is the searchlight platform, and at the top is the maintop, used as a gunnery-spotting station. Above the maintop is a large radio antenna that could be lowered to allow the ship to pass under low bridges. (Library of Congress)

Clad in full-dress uniforms, Rear Admiral Nathaniel R. Usher (left), commandant of the New York Navy Yard, and Captain John D. McDonald, are seen aboard USS *Arizona* on commissioning day. Captain McDonald had been a naval officer for more than three decades, and would command *Arizona* until February 1918. (Library of Congress)

Following the commissioning of USS *Arizona* on 17 October 1916, she was ready for service. At 0800 hours on Friday, 10 November the ship departed the New York Navy Yard and steamed down the East River, the crew standing smartly on deck, as seen here. (National Archives)

Following her maiden voyage, a shakedown cruise that included visits to the Virginia Capes; Newport, Rhode Island; and Guantánamo Bay, Cuba, the *Arizona* returned to New York on 26 December 1916 for further outfitting. In a view taken from the Manhattan Bridge, the ship is seen steaming up the East River *en route* to the New York Navy Yard. In the background are the Brooklyn Bridge and the Manhattan skyline. In honor of the holidays, an evergreen tree was secured to the top of each mast. (Library of Congress)

The fuel-oil-burning *Arizona* (foreground) cruises with coal-burning ships of the U.S. Atlantic Fleet during gunnery practice sometime during her first months in commission. The open bridge aft of the conning tower behind turret two is visible. (Naval History and Heritage Command)

The *Arizona* was photographed at the New York Navy Yard on 3 April 1917, the day of her departure after the completion of turbine repairs and other work in dry dock. The ship was bound for her new home base at the mouth of the York River in Virginia. (National Archives)

In another photo taken from the port quarter of *Arizona* on 3 April 1917, all of the 5-inch/51-caliber guns are still present in the casemates; some of these would be removed during World War I. Atop turret three are three 3-inch 50-caliber antiaircraft guns. (National Archives)

Crewmen perform morning drill on the main deck of the *Arizona* sometime in 1916. Sailors (left) and a USMC detachment (center) double-time around the barbette of turret three while sailors to the right look on. A canvas awning is rigged over the fantail. (WWII Valor in the Pacific National Monument)

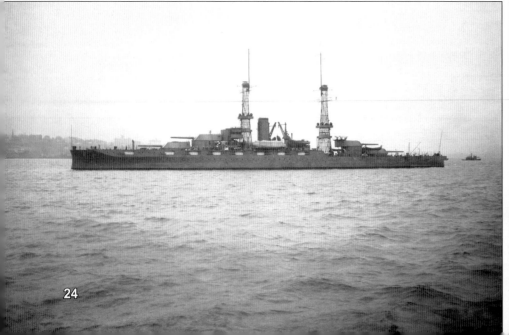

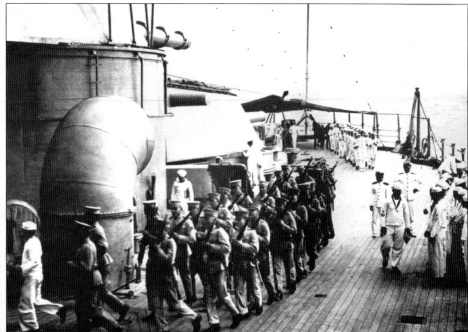

From her aft port quarter at the New York Navy Yard on 3 April 1917, *Arizona* displays her two aft port casemate 5-inch/51-caliber guns. Steel curtains fitted around the casemate guns were intended to keep out seawater, but they were far from waterproof. (National Archives)

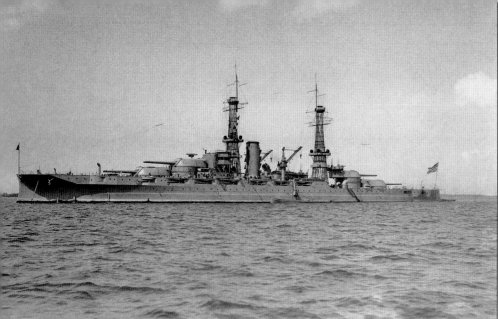

In May 1918 the *Arizona* is based in the York River, functioning as a gunnery training ship. The optical rangefinder atop turret two would be removed in the next few years. The triangular panels affixed to the front of the funnel were designed to make it hard for enemy rangefinders to determine *Arizona's* range and bearing. (National Archives)

By May 1918, the forward-most and the two rear 5-inch/51-caliber casemate guns on each side had been removed to arm cargo vessels. These guns of the secondary battery were to be used against torpedo boats and destroyers. The jack and ensign fly at the bow and stern respectively, U.S. Navy practice for of a ship at anchor. (National Archives)

In the late fall and early winter of 1918, USS *Arizona* made a brief deployment to European waters, during which she assisted in escorting a transport carrying President Woodrow Wilson from Portland, England, to Brest, France. This snapshot shows the ship crossing the English Channel *en route* to Brest. (Naval History and Heritage Command)

Appearing almost ghostlike in the mist, *Arizona* rides at anchor in the North River off Manhattan following her return from Europe on 26 December 1918. Although the *Arizona* had not seen combat during World War I, New York City gave her and other returning warships rousing heroes' welcomes. (Naval History and Heritage Command)

In a view taken from the foretop, sailors man the rails of the *Arizona* to render honors around 1918. The cage masts were made of crisscrossing tubing and were designed to survive direct hits. On the mainmast is the searchlight platform with anti-splinter pads on the guard rails; below it is the aft secondary battery control station. Flanking each side of the mast at the bottom of the photo are the outlines of panels on the deck that could be removed when it was necessary to extricate machinery from within the ship. These panels, known as soft plates, were flush with the deck and planked with teak. (Arizona State Archives)

Sailors were photographed sleeping on deck on the USS *Arizona* while in New York City around 1918. The original caption on this postcard reads, "Before reveille." Sleeping quarters in the ship were stuffy and hot during warm weather, so a more refreshing alternative was to sleep on deck under a canvas awning. (Arizona State Archives)

On the forecastle deck of the *Arizona*, crewmen go about their tasks. Anchor chains are in the foreground. As originally built, the ship had an open bridge aft of the conning tower, both of which are visible above and behind the gun house of turret two. In a modernization in the early 1920s, an enclosed bridge replaced the open one. (WWII Valor in the Pacific National Monument)

In a photograph taken from the foretop of USS *Arizona*, facing forward, while the ship was anchored in the North River off Manhattan in late December 1918, an ice floe encroaches on the bow. Atop the gun house of turret two is an armored optical rangefinder. Within the next two years, the rangefinder would be removed. (Arizona State Archives)

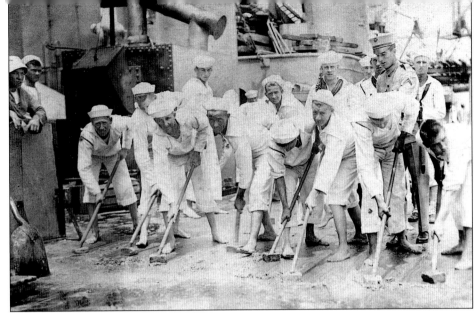

Crewmen of USS *Arizona* holystone the deck. This is a time-honored ritual in the peacetime navy in which the men pushed bricks over sand scattered over the teak deck, rendering it an ashen white. Holystoning was a laborious process; hence, the crew was careful not to mar or scuff the deck, to prolong the interval between holystonings. (Arizona State Archives)

In the days before there were extensive laundry plants in warships, sailors washed their own clothing by hand. This duty was performed topside on the weather deck when conditions allowed it. Crewmen of the USS *Arizona* are seen engaging in this venerable task, using stiff brushes, soap, and galvanized steel buckets full of wash and rinse water. (Arizona State Archives)

Sailors lounge on the main deck of the *Arizona* around 1918. In the background is the feature called the "break of the deck," the transition to the forecastle deck at frame 88. That deck extended from just forward of the mainmast (far right) to the bow. On the left side of the main deck is the port boat crane, to the right of which is stored a motor boat. (Arizona State Archives)

Sailors line-up on the port side of the main deck while a party descends the accommodation ladder to the right. Two officers, one on the grating at the top of the ladder and the other on the ladder, are wearing armbands, probably those of the shore patrol. The shore patrol, or SP, was instrumental in keeping order while the crew was on liberty. (Arizona State Archives)

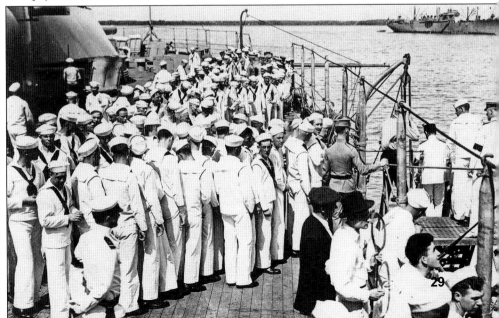

Using portable tables for work surfaces, crewmen on the *Arizona* are laundering clothing. After the garments were washed, they were dried, topside if the weather was fair. Clothes would be hung over the rails, in front of vents, and in any suitable place where the breeze would dry them. When dry, the clothes were ironed, folded, and neatly stored. (Arizona State Archives)

For the morale and health of the crew, physical fitness and recreation were essential. When the USS *Arizona* was at anchor and the weather and sea conditions were suitable, the crew was allowed to go swimming. Here, sailors are diving into the water from the deck while others enjoy a refreshing swim. Sailors to the right watch the activities. (Arizona State Archives)

The USS *Arizona* is in port, and one of the ship's whaleboats on davits along the main deck is being readied for lowering, while sailors look on expectantly. Crewmen would soon be piling into the whaleboat, headed for shore on liberty. There were davits for small boats on each side of the main deck athwart turrets three and four. (Arizona State Archives)

Sailors take advantage of a few spare moments to stretch out on the teak main deck of USS *Arizona*. To the left are turret four and the capstan of a deck winch, while in the background is the starboard boat crane. Running along the outboard edge of the teak deck is the waterway, which served as a gutter to carry off water running off the deck. (WWII Valor in the Pacific National Monument)

Using common brooms, sailors meticulously sweep the main deck of USS *Arizona* adjacent to turret four. Part of the purpose was to keep the men busy, and part was to present a tidy, well maintained battleship. To the left, bedding is hanging over the rail to air out. In the background are a winch, open hatches, ventilators, and the flag staff. (WWII Valor in the Pacific National Monument)

Men of *Arizona's* galley pose beneath some of the ship's boats for a photo to be taken by one of their own. Another man, apparently a Marine, stands to the side holding another camera. *Arizona's* galleys served over 3,000 meals seven days per week, closing only when the ship was in dry dock for overhaul. Mess duty usually fell to seamen first class. (Arizona State Archives)

A boatswain's mate of USS *Arizona* who had traveled 29,447 miles on the ship from 18 November 1918 to 30 June 1919 displays souvenirs he had collected on his voyages, including a stuffed alligator. During that brief period alone, the *Arizona* visited ports of call in England, France twice, New York, Cuba, Trinidad, Turkey, and Gibraltar. (Library of Congress)

Photographed on the North River on 26 December 1918, the *Arizona* is viewed from astern, with flags snapping smartly in the breeze from the radio masts and the mainmast. The 5-inch/51-caliber guns had been removed from the four aft casemates and reassigned to cargo ships, for defense against U-boats during World War I. (Naval History and Heritage Command)

USS *Arizona* rests at anchor off New York City in December 1918 after returning from her deployment to Europe. Secondary-battery director platforms with V-shaped windbreaks had been retrofitted below the searchlight platforms on the mainmast and foremast. (Naval History and Heritage Command)

USS *Arizona* as configured in June 1922

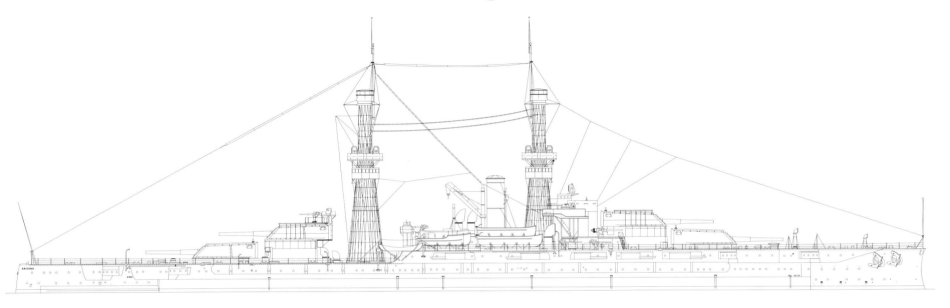

Prior to her 1929-1931 refit, *Arizona* was painted "War Color," a dark slate gray

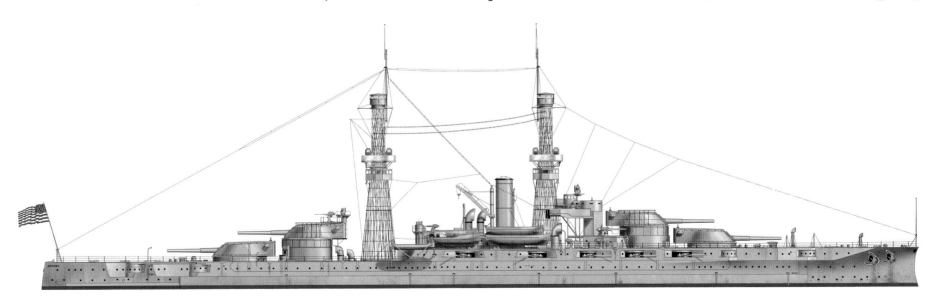

Periodically, the *Arizona* was placed in dry dock for maintenance, repairs, and modifications. As the waters in the dry dock receded, exposing the hull below the waterline, sailors would scrape marine growth from the hull before it dried and became too hard to chip off. The forward port torpedo tube opening, visible in this photograph, was later eliminated. (WWII Valor in the Pacific National Monument)

Crewmen are manhandling a torpedo on a trolley on the deck of the USS *Arizona*. The ship had a torpedo room extending the breadth of the hull below the waterline in the forward part of the ship. The torpedo tubes were fixed and of limited practicality, being effective only in close combat. To the left, a deck winch is being used to pull a line. (WWII Valor in the Pacific National Monument)

USS *Arizona* - General Data, 1916

DIMENSIONS
Length: 608 feet (length overall). 600 feet (waterline length).
Maximum Beam: 97' ½".
Draft: 28' 10" (mean), 29' 10" Maximum (at full load)

CONSTRUCTION
Cost: $7,425,000 (hull and machinery) $12,993,579.23 (total)
Builder: New York Navy Yard, Brooklyn, New York.
Laid Down: 16 March 1914.
Launched: 19 June 1915.
Commissioned: 17 October 1917.

DISPLACEMENT
31,400 tons (standard) 32,567 tons (at full load)

ARMOR PROTECTION
Total Armor Weight: 8,072 tons.
Belt: From frame 20 to 127; 13½" thick for a total eight of 17' 4⅝". From top of second deck to 2' 4" below normal waterline the armor is 13½" thick, tapering uniformly to 8" thick for the 8' 9¾" below waterline. From frame 127 to sternpost: 13" from top of third deck to 2' 4" below normal waterline then tapering at frame 20 through 127.
Ends: Forward at frame 20: 13" between second deck and second platform, tapering to 8" below first platform, for a total depth of 17' 4⅝".
Aft from frame 127: 13" between second and third decks.
Decks: 120-lb protective deck covering armor belt. Splinter deck; 40-lb on flat and 60-lb on slope behind belt.
Turrets: Face plates: 18". Sides: 9", increasing to 10" near the front. Rear: 9". Top: 5".
Exposed undersides: 2".

MACHINERY
Total Weight: 2,462 tons (with liquids).
Boilers: Twelve Babcock & Wilcox; 55,332 square feet total heating surface.
Turbines: Eight Parsons-type turbines on four shafts: Two high-pressure ahead and two high-pressure astern on inboard shafts; two low-pressure ahead and astern and two cruising turbines on outboard shafts. All shafts turn outboard for ahead.
Shaft Horsepower: 34,000 maximum ahead.
Maximum Speed: 21.0 knots at 226 shaft r.p.m.
Generators: Four 300kw, 240-volt DC turbo-generator sets.
Rudders: One, balanced, tapered type; 443-square feet in area. Train limits 38° to port and starboard.
Fuel Oil: 2,332 tons (694,830 gallons).
Reserve Boiler Feed Water: 373.5 tons.
Potable Water: 787.5 tons.
Anchors: Three 20,000-lb each (two to port, one starboard); 180 fathoms chain to port anchors, 120 fathoms to starboard.

COMPLEMENT
1,087 total (including 72 Marines): 56 officers; 1,031 enlisted men.

At Guantánamo Bay, Cuba, in January 1920, USS *Arizona* exhibits a number of modernizations added in 1919, including an enclosed navigation bridge; a 20-foot-coincidence rangefinder on the bridge; aircraft-launching platforms on turrets two and three, and higher searchlight platforms and secondary-battery-director platforms on the masts. (National Archives)

USS *Arizona* is viewed from the aft starboard quarter at Guantánamo Bay in January 1920. In the preceding months, the open secondary-battery-director platforms had been replaced by enclosed director stations of octagonal plan, higher-up on the masts, below the searchlight platforms. A large canvas awning is over the fantail, and a flying-off platform is over turret three. (National Archives)

An oiler is moored to the port side of USS *Arizona* at Guantánamo Bay around 1920. This U.S. naval base, captured during the Spanish-American War, was a frequent port-of-call for the *Arizona* until the ship was transferred to the Pacific Fleet in August 1921. Several boats are moored to the boat boom on the starboard side of *Arizona*. (Naval History and Heritage Command)

A view of battleships lying off Riverside Drive in New York City on 4 May 1920 includes, left to right, USS *Pennsylvania* (BB-38), USS *Arizona* (BB-39), USS *Nevada* (BB-36), and USS *Oklahoma* (BB-37). Visible in this view is the higher navigation bridge of *Arizona*'s sister ship, the *Pennsylvania*, which stood well above the conning tower. (Naval History and Heritage Command)

USS *Arizona* (foreground) and another battleship lie at anchor off Hampton Roads, Virginia, on 22 May 1920. Visible on top of turret two of *Arizona* is the aircraft-launching platform; the forward extension over the 14-inch guns is not installed. The first flight of an aircraft from the *Arizona* occurred at Guantánamo Bay in early 1920. (National Archives)

The USS *Arizona* releases a broadside from her twelve 14-inch/45-caliber main battery in the early 1920s. The concentration dial, or range clock, below the searchlight platform of the mainmast indicates that the guns were firing at a range of about 5,700 yards. The small hand indicated thousands of yards and the big hand hundreds of yards. (Naval History and Heritage Command)

The aft surfaces of the breeches of three of the USS *Arizona's* 14-inch/45-caliber guns are in view. The breech blocks, also called mushroom plugs, pivoted at their bottoms, and were locked in place in the breech with interrupted threads. Powered rammers were used to load the ammunition, comprising projectiles and powder bags, into the breeches. (University of Arizona Library)

Although this photograph was taken aboard USS *Arizona's* sister ship USS *Pennsylvania,* it illustrates a feature that was employed on the *Arizona*. Affixed with clamping bands to the port 14-inch guns of turrets three and four are 1-pounder sub-caliber guns, used as an inexpensive means of simulating short-range trajectories during main-battery exercises. (National Archives)

USS *Arizona* is taking aboard 14-inch projectiles while in port. In addition to the projectiles on the deck, a hoist is lowering a cluster of them. They would then be lowered one by one through hatches to below decks, where they would be stored in magazines and in the ammunition-handling areas of the barbettes. The canvas tarp kept grease on the projectiles from contaminating the teak deck. (University of Arizona Library)

The crew of one of USS *Arizona's* 3-inch/50-caliber antiaircraft guns conducts a firing drill. The ship originally had four of these weapons, and four more were added in 1922. These 3-inch guns would comprise the *Arizona's* sole defenses against aerial attack until the introduction of 5-inch/25-caliber and .50-caliber antiaircraft guns in 1931. (WWII Valor in the Pacific National Monument)

Weapons and Ballistics

Weapon	Ammo Type	Gun Model	Projectile Mark	Projectile Weight	Explosive charge	Muzzle velocity	Range yards
14"/45	Armor Piercing*	3		1,400 lbs	31.5 lbs	2,600 fps	21,000
14"/45	Armor Piercing**	3		1,400 lbs	31.5 lbs	2,700 fps	24,000
14"/45	Armor Piercing	8	20	1,500 lbs	22.9 lbs	2,600 fps	23,000
14"/45	High Capacity	8	19	1,275 lbs	104.2 lbs	2,735 fps	23,500
5"/51	Common	13	15	50 lbs	4.3 lbs	3,150 fps	17,100
5"/51	High Capacity	13	39	50 lbs	26.4 lbs	3,150 fps	17,100
3"/50	APCBC	21	29	13.1 lbs	1.2 lbs	2,700 fps	29,800
3"/50	High Capacity	21	27	13.1 lbs	5.7 lbs	2,700 fps	29,800
3"/50	AAC	21	27	13.1 lbs	5.7 lbs	2,700 fps	29,800

*Data as built, **Data post-modernization

Stripped to their waists and barefooted, the crew of a 5-inch/51-caliber casemate gun conducts a practice drill for loading the piece. At the center, a crouching loader makes ready to insert a projectile into the breech, while to the left, other loaders place powder bags on a loading tray. To the right, a gunner aims the piece. (WWII Valor in the Pacific National Monument)

Discharge water spews from three ports on the side of the hull in this picture taken from close to the starboard side of the bow of USS Arizona in the early 1920s. A good view is provided of the hawse pipes, through which the anchor chains and mooring lines passed. On turret two is the flying-off platform, with the runway visible over the 14-inch guns. (Naval History and Heritage Command)

The port side of USS Arizona is displayed in this undated photograph taken in the early 1920s. Flying-off platforms cast their shadows on the sides of the gun houses of turrets two and three, but the removable runways are not installed over the 14-inch guns. Aft of the funnel are air vents, boat cranes, and stowed boats. Visible to the front of the funnel is the cage mast of a warship in the distance. (National Archives)

USS *Oklahoma* (left) and USS *Arizona* (right) are transiting the Pedro Miguel Locks of the Panama Canal in January 1921. In the far distance is USS *Nevada.* Still assigned to the Atlantic Fleet, these ships were *en route* to the Pacific Ocean for joint tactical maneuvers with ships of the Pacific Fleet off the coast of Peru, held in early February. (Naval History and Heritage Command)

Another photograph of USS *Arizona* in a Panama Canal lock in early 1921 exhibits some of the features of the aft end of the ship. The ship's name was displayed on each side of the stern. Erected over the fantail is a canvas awning that was frequently installed when the ship was in bright, warm climes, to give crewmen some relief from the sun. (Library of Congress)

During her return voyage from joint maneuvers with the Pacific Fleet off Peru, USS *Arizona* transits the Panama Canal on 23 February 1921. Painted on dark-colored bands on the lower parts of turrets two and three were azimuth, or deflection, scales, which enabled other ships in the battle line to ascertain the direction of fire of *Arizona*'s main battery. (Naval History and Heritage Command)

An aerial view of the *Arizona* in the early 1920s shows the awnings set up over several parts of the decks, including form-fitting ones around the mainmast. A large part of the crew is present on deck, with hammocks and bedding laid out for inspection. The azimuth scales are visible on turrets two and three, as are the flying-off platforms on those two turrets. (National Archives)

The flying-off platform is present on turret two, but the runway platform is not installed over that turret's 14-inch guns in this photo of USS *Arizona* dated February 1921. Waving proudly from the jackstaff on the bow is the jack, with white stars on a field of blue. During the *Arizona's* entire service as a warship, she flew a jack with 48 stars. (National Archives)

43

A French-built Nieuport 28 is poised on the flying-off platform atop turret three on the *Arizona* at Guantánamo Bay around 1921, in one of the early experiments at equipping naval ships with their own light aircraft for scouting and liaison duties. A wooden runway, 20 feet wide and a mere 50 feet long, had been erected over the three 14-inch guns. (Naval History and Heritage Command)

Around 1921, a Nieuport fighter takes off from the turret platform (right) on either the USS *Arizona* or USS *Pennsylvania*. To launch the plane, the tail was held secure by a pelican hook while the pilot ran up the engine. With the turret pointed into the wind, the hook was released, and the aircraft shot off the platform and into the air. (Naval History and Heritage Command)

Another photo taken either from the USS *Arizona* or USS *Pennsylvania* shows a Nieuport 28 taking off from the platform on turret three around 1921. The platforms and their supports were made of wood. The legs supporting the runway, located above the 14-inch gun barrels, were attached to bands secured around the gun barrels. (Naval History and Heritage Command)

Visitors pause in front of USS *Arizona's* turret one during the ship's visit to San Francisco in 1923. Tampions are fitted over the 14-inch/45-caliber gun muzzles. At the center and to the extreme right are hatches leading below decks, and on either side of it are ventilators. Above the flying-off platform atop turret three is the aft rangefinder. (WWII Valor in the Pacific National Monument)

At 'em Arizona 1923

Arleigh Burke, an ensign on the *Arizona* and later an admiral and Chief of Naval Operations (CNO), wrote the inscription "At 'em *Arizona* 1923" on the bottom of this snapshot. Painted on the side of the funnel is a large letter E, signifying that the engineering division had won the highest award for efficiency. This is a longtime honor awarded to various divisions on ships of the U.S. fleet. (Naval History and Heritage Command)

The Battle Fleet's war games near the Panama Canal in early 1923 are viewed from the forward port side of USS *Arizona*. In the foreground, turret one is traversed to port, exhibiting a 1-pounder sub-caliber gun mounted on the farthest 14-inch/45-caliber gun. To the extreme right is the port side of turret two and struts for the flying-off platform. (WWII Valor in the Pacific National Monument)

The entire port side of USS *Arizona* is shown in a photograph taken sometime between 1921, when the azimuth scales were painted on turrets two and three, and 1925, when an aircraft catapult was installed on the fantail. Of interest is the box-shaped structure with what appears to be a tall tube above it, on the side of the hull above the boat. (National Archives)

The port amidships section of USS *Arizona* is displayed in a photograph taken on 30 July 1923 while the ship was moored for a week at the Puget Sound Navy Yard, Bremerton, Washington. Four 3-inch/50-caliber antiaircraft guns were installed on the forecastle deck adjacent to the conning tower in 1923; the two port guns are visible here. One of the boats stowed aft of the funnel is prominently marked "ARIZ" on its bow. (Puget Sound Naval Shipyard)

In early 1924, USS *Arizona* briefly left the Pacific and returned to the Caribbean and Atlantic. During this voyage, the ship was largely engaged in exercises at the gunnery range at Culebra Island, Puerto Rico. Here, the *Arizona* is seen at anchor with other ships of the Scouting Force in Guantánamo Bay. To the left is USS *Mahan* (DD-102). (Naval History and Heritage Command)

Barely visible in the darkness are two warships, including what is believed to be the USS *Arizona* to the right of center, illuminated at Piers 8 and 9 at Honolulu during a U.S. fleet celebration for the citizens of that city in the 1920s. Fleet celebrations were intended to build good relations between the navy and the ports that hosted naval facilities. (Naval History and Heritage Command)

Crewmen hoist USS *Arizona's* first floatplane, a Vought UO-1, onto the fantail at San Pedro, California, in early 1925. The plane's bureau number, A6604, is on the vertical fin. On the deck is a dolly, onto which the center pontoon of the aircraft will be positioned. A catapult would later be installed on the fantail of the ship in the summer of 1925. (WWII Valor in the Pacific National Monument)

In the late 1920s, several Vought O2U Corsair scout/observation floatplanes were assigned to USS *Arizona*. First ordered by the U.S. Navy in 1927, the O2U Corsair had a crew of two and a maximum range of approximately 680 miles. Here, a crane on a fleet oiler delivers an 02U to the USS *Arizona* while another O2U with side number 3/6 sits on deck. (WWII Valor in the Pacific National Monument)

USS *Arizona* rides at anchor at Honolulu on 3 May 1925 following firing exercises with the Battle Fleet off Haleina, Oahu. Of interest is the huge awning extending from forward of the main mast, enclosing barbette three and covering turret four. The letter E on the funnel and the azimuth scales on the turrets-two and -three gun houses were still present. (National Archives)

The bow is to the right in this image taken from 1,000 feet over the USS *Arizona* off Honolulu on 6 May 1925. Visible in this photo and the preceding one is the circular base for a catapult on the fantail. The remainder of the catapult would be installed at the Puget Sound Naval Ship Yard, Bremerton, Washington, during an overhaul that summer. (National Archives)

A rear admiral conducts an inspection on the deck of USS *Arizona*. Reportedly, Captain Percy Olmsted, commander of the ship from 1923 to 1925, is behind the rear admiral. Sailors have laid out their hammocks and bedding for inspection. To the lower left are members of the ship's band. Behind the ventilator to the left are turrets three and four. (WWII Valor in the Pacific National Monument)

USS *Arizona* passes through the Miraflores Locks of the Panama Canal in the mid-1920s. With her 97-foot beam, *Arizona* had 13 feet of freeboard in the 110-foot-wide locks. Awnings were erected to give the crewmen on the deck some relief from the scorching sun. The flying-off platform on turret two had been removed by this point. (Naval History and Heritage Command)

The *Arizona* rides at anchor in the North River (or lower Hudson River) off Manhattan on 2 May 1927. Two floatplanes are on the fantail: one on the catapult and the other on the deck. This catapult was mounted to the port of the centerline of the ship. The box-like structure forward of the mainmast is thought to have been an aviation-related compartment. (National Archives)

USS *Arizona* conducts exercises with other warships of the U.S. fleet. Two scout/observation floatplanes are stored on the fantail catapult. Light-colored curtains present on the openings of the casemates were intended to keep out water, but they would often fail in high seas. The dark "splotch" on the side of the hull is a shadow cast by a boat. (Naval History and Heritage Command)

Flying all signal flags from stem to stern, the USS *Arizona* is dressed for a special occasion. This view displays details of the forecastle, including anchor chains, two open hatches, and a ventilator. Above turret two is the top of the conning tower, with its vision slits faintly visible, and above the conning tower is the enclosed bridge.

Biplanes fly over USS *Arizona* on 4 June 1927, the date on which the *Arizona* and other ships of the fleet passed in review for President Calvin Coolidge at Hampton Roads, Virginia. On the funnel is a large letter E, symbolic of the award for efficiency the ship's engineering department won in July 1926: a much-coveted honor in the U.S. Navy. (National Archives)

An aerial photograph of USS *Arizona*, with sailors manning the rails, was taken from one of the aircraft flying over the ship during President Coolidge's review on 4 June 1927. A close examination of the photo reveals two 3-inch/50-caliber antiaircraft guns on top of turret three, and a dark-colored captain's gig next to the starboard boat crane. (National Archives)

In another aerial photo of the *Arizona* during the President Coolidge's review at Hampton Roads, two floatplanes are stored on the fantail catapult, in tandem order: an arrangement that was sometimes observed. When it was necessary to launch an aircraft from the catapult, the forward plane would be lowered onto a dolly and secured to the deck. (National Archives)

On 3 February 1928, USS *Arizona* is docked at Navy Yard Puget Sound, undergoing upgrades and maintenance. The catapult has been removed from the fantail, exposing the catapult's circular mount. The antiquated vessel to the upper right was Crane Ship Number 1, formerly USS *Kearsarge* (BB-5). To the top left is the oiler USS *Neches* (AO-5). (Puget Sound Naval Shipyard)

The *Arizona* undergoes modernization in dry dock at Norfolk Navy Yard in Portsmouth, Virginia. During the rebuild the cage masts were replaced with tripod masts, the superstructure virtually replaced, and the secondary armament reconfigured. (University of Arizona Library)

Modernization, 1929-1931

The USS *Arizona* underwent a modernization program involving numerous modifications in compliance with the terms of the Washington Naval Limits Treaty at Norfolk Navy Yard, between May 1929 and March 1931. Her cage masts were removed, and tripod-type mainmast and foremast were installed, each of which was topped with a secondary battery control station, air-defense station, and main-battery gun director; these structures were called control tops. Two additional inches of armor were added to the second deck, and anti-torpedo bulges were installed on the hull.

The entire superstructure was completely razed and a replaced with a redesigned one that included an admiral's bridge, a charthouse, and a pilothouse. A new funnel was erected. The 5-inch/51-caliber casemate guns below the weather deck were removed. Ten of those guns were moved to new casemates on the lower level of the superstructure, and two of them were relocated atop the superstructure deck next to the conning tower. A new antiaircraft battery of eight 5-inch/25-caliber guns was installed on the superstructure deck level.

Other modifications implemented during the 1929-1931 modernization included the replacement of the compressed-air catapult on the stern with a powder-operated catapult, the installation of a fixed powder catapult atop turret three, the upgrading of the engines and turbogenerators, and installation of new boilers.

Engines and machinery originally fitted in the never-completed Colorado-class battleship *Washington* (BB-47) were now pulled out of storage and installed in *Arizona*.

A stripped-down USS *Arizona* undergoes modernization at Norfolk Navy Yard. (U.S. Navy)

During modernization, the mainmast of the *Arizona* is viewed from the foremast. Previously, at least one publication has identified this as the foremast, but the four ventilators at the bottom mark this as the mainmast. The aft secondary battery control station and, over it, the aft air-defense station are taking shape at the top of the mast. The main battery gun director will later be added to the top. (WWII Valor in the Pacific National Monument)

Only a few months from the completion of its modernization, USS *Arizona* sits at dock at Norfolk in December 1930, with the destroyer USS *Cole* (DD-155) in the background. One of the modifications implemented during this work was the enlargement of the gun apertures in the main-battery gun houses. The larger apertures allowed the 14-inch/45-caliber guns to elevate 30 degrees in unison: a marked improvement over their original 15 degrees of elevation. Several of the relocated secondary-battery 5-inch/51-caliber guns are visible in the casemates on the lower level of the superstructure. (Michael W. Pocock collection)

In 1926 the General Board of the United States Navy had recommended that seven U.S. battleships be reconstructed. This reconstruction would involve their conversion from coal-burning to oil-fired vessels; increase the elevation of their main guns, allowing greater range; and enhance their protection against torpedo and air attacks. The vessels recommended for reconstruction were the battleships *Nevada, Oklahoma, Pennsylvania, Arizona, New Mexico, Mississippi,* and *Idaho.* East Coast navy yards were selected for this work, in part because the West Coast navy yards at that time were being kept busy maintaining the newly expanded Pacific Fleet.

The rebuilding effort was divided up between two East Coast yards, with Philadelphia Navy Yard modernizing *Oklahoma, Pennsylvania,* and *New Mexico,* and the Norfolk Navy Yard, in Virginia, handling the remainder of the battlewagons. All work was performed on a rotation basis, so that the ships were not all withdrawn from service simultaneously.

Arizona began her refit in May 1929, five months prior to Black Tuesday and the start of the Great Depression in the United States. In the following months, the $5.29 million spent on *Arizona's* modernization, as well as the similar cost of the successive modernization of *Mississippi* (work done 30 March 1931 through September 1933) and *Idaho,* (work done 30 September 1930 through 9 October 1934), provided an important influx of money into the state of Virginia. Such was the importance of this work at that time that it was featured on numerous tourist and promotional items – all of which, like anything vintage USS *Arizona,* are highly collectible today.

The photograph of USS *Arizona* during its modernization with USS *Cole* in the background was also a popular subject for postcards, as evidenced by these two examples, including a colorized version. The ships were not identified by name: the more important but unspoken theme of these highly collectible souvenirs seems to have been that the ongoing work at the navy yards was giving a tremendous boost to the depression-wracked economy. These postcards also would have found a ready market among sailors assigned to the two ships. (Marcus Robbins collection)

Poster stamps were similar in size and appearance to postage stamps, but were in effect miniaturized posters, issued for promotional purposes. This poster stamp of USS *Arizona* was based on the same photograph as the preceding illustration, showing the USS *Cole* in the background. The stamp was issued to promote Virginia's seashores.

During the ship's modernization, *Arizona's* hull has been fitted with torpedo-defense bulges, incorporating oil-filled and air-filled compartments designed to absorb the shock of a torpedo explosion. The tops of the bulges were even with the tops of the belt armor. The result was the widened hull at the waterline seen here. The hull was now 106 feet 2¾ inches wide, a gain of over nine feet. (National Archives)

A view from the starboard beam illustrates the new superstructure, funnel, and tripod masts. The fighting tops atop the masts had three levels, comprising, from top to bottom, the main-battery gun director, air-defense station, and secondary-battery control station. Also present on the mainmast were platforms for .50-caliber machine guns and a rangefinder platform. (National Archives)

Still moored to the dock at Norfolk Navy Yard on 2 March 1931, USS *Arizona's* modernization is now complete. The following day she would depart Norfolk to begin trials. The elongated gun apertures of the main-battery gun houses are clearly visible. Above the conning tower is the chart house, with four round portholes; above that is the pilot house. (National Archives)

The secondary-battery casemate mounts below the weather decks were eliminated during modernization and the openings covered with steel plates. These gun positions, primarily intended to defend against torpedo attacks by enemy destroyers, had proved to be wet in heavy seas and were too low to allow accurate and effective firing. (National Archives)

On 2 March 1931, the catapult on the fantail is present, but the catapult on turret three is not installed. The aircraft boom at the stern dated to the late 1920s and would later be replaced by a more substantial crane. The boat cranes were moved aft to the break of the deck, and their booms were extended so they could lift aircraft to the turret catapult. (National Archives)

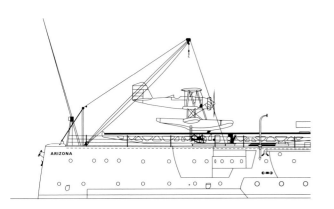

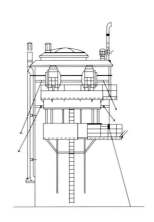

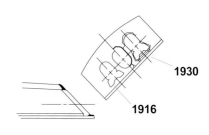

A catapult was installed on the stern of *Arizona* as part of her 1929-1931 modernization. A simple boom pole, seen here in its 1931-1934 configuration, served the catapult until 1934, when a more substantial crane was installed.

This illustration indicates the position of *Arizona's* searchlights and funnel prior to the shipyard work, conducted from December 1935 through February 1936, in the course of which the funnel height was increased.

During the 1929-1931 modernization of USS *Arizona,* her main battery turret faceplates were changed in order to allow the guns to elevate 30°, an increase of 15° over their original configuration.

USS *Arizona* in her March 1936 configuration

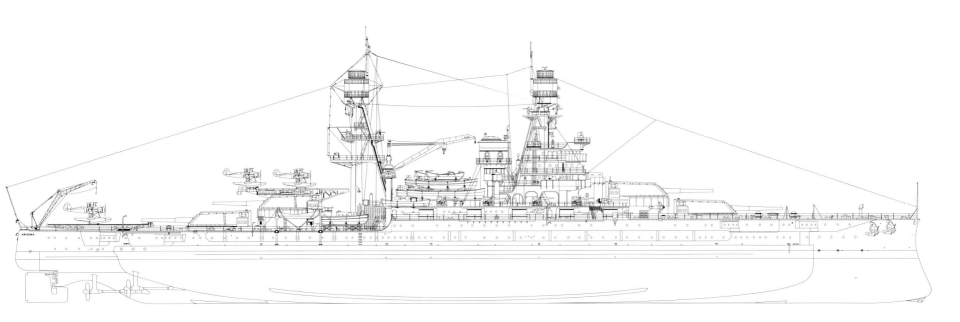

This is one of eight 5-inch/25-caliber Mk. 11 semiautomatic antiaircraft guns on single Mk. 19 mounts installed on the superstructure deck level of USS *Arizona* during the 1929-1931 modernization. The gun, intended to defend against long-range aerial targets, also could be used against surface targets. The crew was entirely exposed. (University of Arizona Library)

USS *Arizona* is underway in early 1931, following her 1929-1931 modernization. The catapult has yet to be mounted atop the gun house of turret three. Crewmen are manning the rails, signifying that the ship was passing in review before a VIP or about to take one on board. The new positions of the boat cranes at the break of the deck are apparent. (National Archives)

M. C. Matthews of USS *Arizona's* race-boat team poses next to a 5-inch/25-caliber gun with a tampion with a star decoration inserted in the muzzle. Boat-racing was a popular activity when the ship was in port, where her crew would compete against crews from other ships of the fleet. The *Arizona's* race-boat teams won a number of coveted trophies. (WWII Valor in the Pacific National Monument)

A few days after the USS *Arizona* completed its modernization program, the ship received news that President Herbert Hoover was going to take a vacation trip to the Caribbean aboard her. Hoover boarded the *Arizona* on 19 March 1931. The ship is seen here during the cruise. (National Archives)

In an aerial view of USS *Arizona* from aft, the Vought O3U Corsair floatplane (not to be confused with the Vought F4U Corsair of World War II) stored on the main deck adjacent to turret three is fully visible. Shortly after this cruise, a second catapult would be installed on top of the gun house of turret three, designated Type P (for Powder) Mk. IV Mod 1. (Naval History and Heritage Command)

This shot of the *Arizona* from astern was also taken by an aircraft from Langley Field on 29 March 1931. A Vought O3U floatplane is on the fantail catapult, which was designated the Type P Mk. V (or simply the P-5), while another O3U rests on the main deck to the forward port quarter of turret three. Typically, three scout/observation float planes were carried aboard. (National Archives)

Part of the crew assembles along the fantail catapult during President Hoover's cruise. A close inspection of the photo indicates that the starboard boat crane has hoisted a captain's gig and is either bringing it back onboard or is about to lower it into the water. Forward of the main mast is a collection of boats, stored on deck in a stacked fashion. (National Archives)

In still another photo taken by the Langley Field Photo Section, the two Vought O3U Corsair scout/observation planes are shown in closer detail. The catapult was actuated by a special brass powder cartridge. A gunnery officer would supervise the launching, making sure the ship's stern was moving in an upward direction at the moment of launch. (Naval History and Heritage Command)

The USS *Arizona* was photographed from an aircraft of the Langley Field, Virginia, Photo Section on 29 March 1931 while President Hoover was aboard. Details visible include the optical rangefinder atop the pilot house, and a paravane, a towed anti-mine device, on each side of the barbette of turret two (the starboard paravane is in shadows). The secondary guns, like the main battery, are stowed oriented parallel to the keel, standard practice aboard *Arizona* when the weapons were secured. (National Archives)

Captain Charles S. Freeman, commander of USS *Arizona*, fourth from left and next to President Hoover, hosted a formal dinner on the quarterdeck for the honored guest during the March 1931 cruise, which included visits to Puerto Rico and the Virgin Islands. Details of the markings of one of the Vought O3U aircraft are visible. (Naval History and Heritage Command)

President Hoover visits the forward part of the navigation bridge, with an engine-order telegraph (EOT) to the right. Hoover's Caribbean cruise came at a time when his popularity was low, and he was finding it difficult to lead the country through the dark days of the Great Depression. He spent much of the voyage reading mystery novels. (National Archives)

President Hoover receives a tutorial on the operation of an antiaircraft rangefinder. In the 1929-1931 modernization, two antiaircraft rangefinders were placed on the platform over the navigation bridge, on either side of the foremast. The rangefinder included a horizontal optical tube assembly and a vertical tube that served to calculate the slant range to an enemy aircraft. (National Archives)

During President Hoover's cruise on the *Arizona* on Sunday, 22 March 1931, his presidential standard waves from the maintop, while a church pennant flies over the national flag. A good view is provided of the aft concentration dial, the framing underneath the control top and the cloverleaf platform, and the mass of electrical conduits. (National Archives)

President Hoover's vacation cruise on USS *Arizona* began and concluded at Hampton Roads, Virginia. The ship is seen with the presidential standard flying from the main mast at Hampton Roads off Old Point Comfort; the large building with the twin towers in the background is the landmark Chamberlin Hotel, which still survives. (National Archives)

On 16 July 1931, only four months after completion of its modernization, USS *Arizona* went into drydock at the South Boston Navy Yard Annex for five days to undergo turbine repairs. As shown here, as the waters in the drydock receded, crewmen worked quickly to scrape barnacles and other deposits from the hull before the air caused them to harden. (Naval History and Heritage Command)

The *Arizona* is viewed from off the bow in drydock at the South Boston Navy Yard Annex in July 1931. Once the ship entered the drydock, huge gates were shut to close off the basin, and the water in it was removed by powerful pumps in a pump house. Once repairs on the ship were complete, the water was let back in drydock and the ship departed. (Naval History and Heritage Command)

USS *Arizona* rests on the bottom of a drydock at Pearl Harbor on 2 March 1932, the completely exposed lower hull thoroughly braced. Crewmen on scaffolding work on the stern below the waterline. The massive rudder and several of the propellers are visible, and the aft edge of the anti-torpedo bulge is above the leftmost propeller. (Naval History and Heritage Command)

After spending the winter of 1931-1932 based at San Pedro, California, USS *Arizona* steamed to Hawaii in February 1932 and went into drydock at Pearl Harbor, Oahu, on 2 March 1932, where the ship was photographed from the air the following day. Although the ship had visited Honolulu before, this was her first visit to Pearl Harbor. (National Archives)

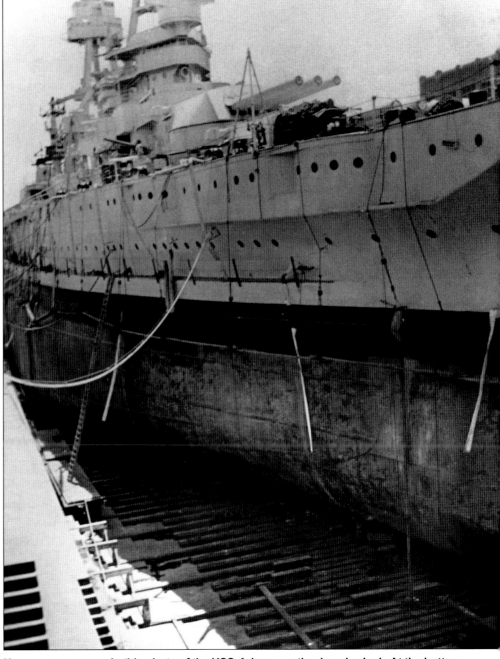

No crewmen appear in this photo of the USS *Arizona* resting in a drydock. At the bottom of the drydock basin are the wooden beams and blocks that supported the hull of the ship after the water was pumped from the basin. Along the waterline of the hull is a black band called the boot topping, designed to hide smudges from oil floating in harbors; below that band, the hull was painted with red lead. (Naval History and Heritage Command)

67

The 14-inch/45-caliber guns of turrets one through three, and probably four, are elevated, with turrets three and four traversed to the port side. Present on turret three is the catapult installed soon after President Hoover's Caribbean cruise in early 1931. The aircraft crane on the fantail was replaced by a more substantial crane in mid-1934. (National Archives)

Her bow almost disappearing below the surface, the USS *Arizona* crashes through heavy waves *en route* from San Pedro, California, to San Francisco in late April 1932. During that trip, the *Arizona* conducted tactical maneuvers with other ships of the fleet. In the left background, the foretop and foremast of the USS *Nevada* can be seen. (National Archives)

USS *Arizona* is shown in one of her periodic visits to drydock for maintenance and repairs at Pearl Harbor in 1932. Hawsers have been secured from the sides of the drydock to the ship, to keep her centered as the water recedes. Men are beginning to bring boats to the sides of the hull, to begin scraping marine growth as the water subsides. (WWII Valor in the Pacific National Monument)

Here Comes the Navy

Since 7 December 1941, USS *Arizona* has featured in countless films, but her first "starring role" came in much happier times. Warner Brothers filmed much of *Here Comes the Navy*, a romantic comedy starring James Cagney, Pat O'Brien, and Gloria Stuart, aboard *Arizona* off San Diego, California. While many today might consider the plot line of the film to be corny, it remains a very "clean" movie, suited for viewers of all ages, and it provides rare insights into the life of sailors aboard *Arizona* in March 1934, when the movie was filmed.

While the movie "leads" were actors, *Arizona's* crew serve as "extras," while going about their daily routines. A studio-produced mock-up was used in filming most of the main battery turret interior scenes, but otherwise, the movie features many glimpses of the interior and exterior of the spotless *Arizona*. Scenes of the *Arizona* firing her 14-inch main battery during maneuvers are also included. Some of this footage was shot from the Navy's giant "flying aircraft carrier," the airship USS *Macon*. *Macon* herself is featured in the later portion of the film, after the movie's leading men have been transferred to her from *Arizona*. *Macon* was lost at sea less than a year after the filming. *Here Comes the Navy* was first screened aboard the *Arizona* on 30 July 1934, understandably to the delight of the crew, many of whom made sport of spotting themselves or their friends on screen.

In a production still from *Here Comes the Navy*, James Cagney discusses a point with his costar, Gloria Stuart, with the USS *Arizona* looming in the background, turret two traversed to starboard. Just four months after the filming, the men of the *Arizona* got their first look at the finished movie during an onboard screening on 30 July 1934.

While based at San Pedro, California, in the spring of 1934, USS *Arizona* served as a location for *Here Comes the Navy*, a Warner Brothers comedy starring James Cagney. The ship was featured in many scenes, and the film includes priceless footage of the ship along with her crew engaged in their daily routines. Shown here is a poster for the movie.

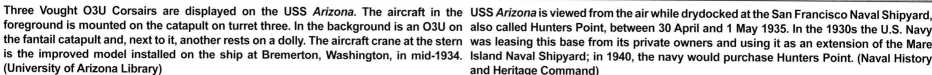

Three Vought O3U Corsairs are displayed on the USS *Arizona*. The aircraft in the foreground is mounted on the catapult on turret three. In the background is an O3U on the fantail catapult and, next to it, another rests on a dolly. The aircraft crane at the stern is the improved model installed on the ship at Bremerton, Washington, in mid-1934. (University of Arizona Library)

USS *Arizona* is viewed from the air while drydocked at the San Francisco Naval Shipyard, also called Hunters Point, between 30 April and 1 May 1935. In the 1930s the U.S. Navy was leasing this base from its private owners and using it as an extension of the Mare Island Naval Shipyard; in 1940, the navy would purchase Hunters Point. (Naval History and Heritage Command)

This photograph of USS *Arizona* dates to April 1935. During the first three weeks of that month, the ship was anchored at San Pedro, California. The ship spent the last week of April 1935 steaming to San Francisco, where she arrived on the 30th of the month. Several boats of various sizes and types are moored to the battleship. (National Archives)

The forward part of USS *Arizona's* mainmast is viewed from the forward control top in the last half of the 1930s. At the bottom is a cloverleaf platform for four Browning .50-caliber antiaircraft machine guns. To the lower right is a Curtiss SOC Seagull, a type of float plane that replaced the Vought O3U Corsair on the *Arizona* in 1935. (University of Arizona Library)

The stepped top of the armored belt and the anti-torpedo bulge is quite pronounced along the hull above the waterline in this view of the USS *Arizona* at San Pedro on 18 April 1935. The space saved by the installation of new, more compact boilers in the 1929-1931 modernization also freed up space for additional anti-torpedo compartments in the hull. (National Archives)

The *Arizona* displays her 1934-1936 configuration in this photo taken on 23 August 1935. The funnel seen here was installed during the ship's 1929-1931 modernization. In 1936, the top of the funnel would be extended, to carry fumes from the uptakes away from the pilothouse and other compartments in the upper part of the superstructure. (National Archives)

USS *Arizona* cuts a fine figure as she proceeds through San Francisco Bay in the mid-1930s. Faintly visible on top of turret two is the number 9: the ship's BB number, 39, was painted on the gun house roof at this time, as an identification aid for friendly aircraft. The number was oriented with the tops of the numerals toward the front. (National Archives)

The *Arizona* is moored at the Puget Sound Navy Yard, Bremerton, Washington, on 14 February 1936, having completed a three-month renovation program that included extending the top of the funnel. The white bucklers (the boots sealing the openings around the 14-inch guns) seen in the preceding photo had been replaced by black bucklers. (Puget Sound Naval Shipyard)

Battleships of the U.S. Navy, including USS *Arizona* to the left, are viewed from astern during an ocean crossing. A close inspection of the photograph reveals scout/observation planes mounted on the fantail catapult, the third-turret catapult, and to the port side of the fantail catapult. To the right is a ship that still retains its cage masts. (National Archives, San Francisco, via Tracy White)

Huge waves buffet the *Arizona* during a Pacific crossing in August 1936. During such conditions, the main deck would frequently be awash, and, although the casemate guns had been moved up one level during the 1929-1931 modernization, the casemate compartments often took on water when big waves battered the ship. (National Archives, San Francisco, via Tracy White)

The *Arizona* is viewed from her aft port quarter. The extended top of the funnel, a 1936 modification, is apparent. The catapult on turret three was oriented to launch aircraft over the rear of the turret. Unlike the fantail catapult, which pivoted, the turret catapult was fixed to the turret, with the turret being traversed to achieve the desired catapult position. (National Archives)

Scout/observation-plane operations, all apparently involving Vought O3U-3s, are underway in this photo of USS *Arizona*. Above turret one is a floatplane in flight. On the ship, the port boat/aircraft crane is lowering a floatplane onto the catapult on turret three, and the stern crane is positioning another floatplane over the fantail catapult. (National Archives)

USS *Arizona* displays her aft starboard quarter during the last half of the 1930s. Three of the four 36-inch searchlights are visible on platforms on the sides of the funnel. These lights had been located there since the 1929-1931 modernization. In 1939 the four searchlights would be moved to the cloverleaf platform on the mainmast. (National Archives)

During the 1930s the USS *Arizona* underwent a number of refurbishments and modifications at the Puget Sound Naval Shipyard at Bremerton, Washington. The ship is seen during one such visit on 2 August 1937. The *Arizona* appears to be in an unusually bright and clean condition, suggesting she received a complete repaint at the shipyard. (Puget Sound Naval Shipyard)

Once turret four was removed from its barbette, it was temporarily stored on a foundation constructed of wooden timbers. The front of the gun house, with the faceplate removed, is visible at the top of the turret assembly. The faceplate consisted of 18 inches of armor, while the sides were protected by nine inches of armor. Five inches of armor protected the turret roof. Each turret weighed between 714 and 724 tons. When in place, the turret's machinery could rotate the massive structure at a rate of two degrees per second throughout an arc of +150° to -150°. The levels of the turret below the gun house contained areas for ammunition handing and mechanisms for operating the turret. (Naval Sea Systems Command)

The *Arizona* returned to Bremerton in late May 1938 for maintenance, including the temporary removal of turret four, apparently in order to make repairs or modifications to the interior of the turret or its mounting. Before removal of the turret from the barbette, the 14-inch guns, along with the front and roof of the gun house, were removed. (Naval Sea Systems Command)

Turret four has just been lifted clear of its barbette, at the lower left, on 23 May 1938. The sides of the gun house are visible at the top of the turret. In the background are turret three, traversed to the port side, and the mainmast, flanked by the boat/aircraft cranes. Below the cloverleaf platform on the mainmast is the aft 12-foot optical rangefinder. (Naval Sea Systems Command)

USS *Arizona* - Post-Modernization Data

DIMENSIONS
Length: 608' 0" Overall; 600' 0" Waterline
Maximum Beam: 106' 2¾"
Draft: 28' 10" Mean; 30' 1¾" Full Load; 33' 3" Emergency Load.

DISPLACEMENT
34,207 tons Normal; 32,600 tons Standard (Washington Treaty Measurement); 37,654 tons Full Load (trial 1931)

ARMOR PROTECTION
Armor: As built, except for addition of 70lb. STS horizontal plating (approx. 1.7") to the second deck as bomb protection and an armored grating inside the funnel at the upper deck level.

MACHINERY
Boilers: Six Bureau Express-type; 300-psi/472° F. operating temperature.
Turbines: Four Westinghouse geared Impulse/Reaction 3,600 RPM High Pressure Main Turbines; Four Westinghouse geared Impulse/Reaction 3,600 RPM cruise turbines; Four Parsons 226 RPM Low Pressure ahead and astern turbines; Four Parsons 226 RPM High Pressure astern turbines.
Shaft Horsepower: 35,081 maximum ahead.
Maximum Speed: 20.7 knots.
Generators: Four 300kw 120/240-volt DC turbo-generator sets.
Propellers: Four three-bladed, 12' 7" diameter.
Fuel Oil: 4,630 tons normal/6,180 tons emergency.
Reserve Boiler Feed Water: 323 tons normal, plus 392 tons added emergency capacity.

COMPLEMENT
1,731 total (92 officers and warrants; 1,639 enlisted men).

USS *Arizona* was once again in Bremerton on 30 March 1939, when this view of her starboard side was taken. The four 36-inch searchlights had been removed from the platforms on the sides of the funnel and mounted on the cloverleaf platform on the mainmast. Two .50-caliber machine guns would be mounted on the former searchlight platforms. (Puget Sound Naval Shipyard)

USS *Arizona* rides at anchor off Seattle in the late 1930s. A clear view is offered of the crane. On the fantail catapult is a Curtiss SOC-3 Seagull, a type of scout/observation floatplane that entered service with the U.S. Navy in 1935. Two accommodation ladders are installed on the side of the hull, and the admiral's barge is moored to a boat boom. (Puget Sound Maritime Historical Society)

Two of USS *Arizona's* Curtiss SOC-3 Seagulls appear in this 1939 photograph. Covers are fitted over the cockpit canopies. The first number in the unit/aircraft markings on the aircraft, 1, stood for Observation Squadron 1 (VO-1). The *Arizona* was assigned aircraft numbers 1-O-1 to 1-O-3. Other markings included "U.S. Navy," "U.S.S. *Arizona*," the bureau numbers, and "SOC-3." (WWII Valor in the Pacific National Monument)

Aviation and the *Arizona*

For the strategists of the "battleship navy," the greatest use of an aircraft was to serve as the eyes of the ship. In their minds, the big guns were the decisive armament of a navy, and as the weapons' ranges continued to increase, it became increasingly difficult to adjust their aim. Direct observation of shell fall was the means by which aim was corrected. As built, *Arizona's* big guns could reach out up to 24,000 yards – during her modernization the mountings were modified to increase the maximum elevation from 15 to 30 degrees, and the maximum range up to 34,000 yards – a range beyond which the spotters atop the masts could see. Hence, aircraft were considered a vital part of the ships' fire control system, carrying the spotters aloft and over the enemy.

While flying-off platforms had been installed in January of 1920, these awkward stations permitted only the launching, but not the recovery, of the ship's Nieuport and Sopwith biplanes, which had to rely on being able to return to land, or ditching at sea to end their flight. In 1925 her first catapult was installed on the stern, permitting the launching and recovery of floatplanes. A second catapult was installed atop turret three during her 1929-1931 reconstruction. In 1934 a more substantial stern crane was installed. Over the years of her career, the *Arizona* embarked a variety of aircraft, from the early, land-type airplanes to (in chronological order): the Vought UO-1, Vought O2U and O3U Corsairs, Curtiss SOC-3 Seagulls (as at left), and finally Vought OS2U-1 and OS2U-3 Kingfishers.

The central galley of the USS *Arizona,* seen in this 1930s photograph, was located amidships aft of the funnel on the forecastle deck and was where food for the ship's various messes was cooked. Overhead are ventilator ducts. Food preparation tables are present, and to the right are urns for preparing hot drinks. (WWII Valor in the Pacific National Monument)

Crewmen's hammocks hang over the deck of USS *Arizona* to air out in the late 1930s. During this period, enlisted men still slept on the venerable hammock. Often these were rigged in the gun casemates, and the men slept in the same spaces as their mess halls. During the day, the hammocks were rolled up and stowed in bins called hammock netting. (WWII Valor in the Pacific National Monument)

Two battleships, the USS *Arizona* in the background and probably the USS *New Mexico* (BB-40) in the foreground, are underway in the Pacific near the Hawaiian Islands in September 1940. During that month, the *Arizona* engaged in exercises in Hawaiian waters and then sailed eastward to Long Beach, California. (Getty Images)

In October 1940, USS *Arizona* made her final maintenance-and-repair trip to Navy Yard Puget Sound, where she was photographed next to USS *Nevada* on 18 January 1941, the day before she departed. The ship was painted overall in #5 Standard Navy Gray. A prominent modification made during that stay was the "birdbath" gun tub atop the maintop, with four Browning .50-caliber antiaircraft machine guns. (Puget Sound Naval Shipyard)

The *Arizona* is partially visible through a maze of cranes and boats at the Puget Sound Navy Yard in late 1940 or early 1941. To the right of the crane at the far left is turret two, while next to the top of the boom of the crane at the center is the foretop. To the right of that crane is the mainmast, with turrets three and four to the right. (Tracy White collection)

The mainmast of USS *Arizona* rises to the left at Puget Sound Navy Yard. Other modifications to the ship at that base in 1940-1941 included the addition of splinter shields for the guns on the weather decks and emplacements for four quad 1.1-inch antiaircraft guns (which were never installed). Visible in the background at the center is the USS *Enterprise* (CV-6). (Tracy White collection)

USS *Arizona* traded its SOC-3s for Vought OS2U-1 Kingfisher scout/observation floatplanes in early 1941. One Kingfisher rests on a dolly on the fantail while another approaches the recovery sled that the ship is towing. The sled was used to haul the floatplane alongside the ship so the crane could hoist it onboard. By the time of the attack on Pearl Harbor, the *Arizona* carried OS2U-3 Kingfishers. (National Archives)

The OS2U on the water has engaged the net-covered sled with a hook on the bottom of its center pontoon, and the sled – and the Kingfisher – are being reeled in. To the left, the stern crane is ready to hoist the aircraft aboard. This method of reeling in the aircraft was called the cast method. On the catapult, the launch cart is ready for remounting the floatplane. (National Archives)

A Vought OS2U Kingfisher taxis on a calm area after landing. The recovery sled, to its left, carries two small red flags, for extra visibility. If the ocean was rough during an aircraft recovery operation, a calm area of water could be created by turning the ship; this action temporarily stilled the waters within the curve of the turn. (National Archives)

As an OS2U approaches a recovery sled, rigging from the aircraft crane dangles in the foreground. The OS2U carried a crew of two: the pilot and, in the rear seat, an observer/radio operator who also operated a defensive .30-caliber machine gun. The plane could carry underwing 100- or 250-pound bombs or 325-pound depth charges. (National Archives)

This OS2U Kingfisher carries the unit markings for Observation Squadron 1 (VO-1), which was assigned to Battle Division 1, comprising USS *Arizona*, USS *Nevada*, and USS *Pennsylvania*. The unit markings, or side number, comprised the number 1 for the squadron, the letter O for Observation, and the number 3 for the plane's sequential number. (National Archives)

The recovery sled has assisted this OS2U Kingfisher of VO-1 to come alongside USS *Arizona*, and the observer/radio operator has scrambled onto the starboard wing to grapple the hook from the aircraft crane. Once the crewman grabbed the hook, he would secure it to a fastener on the turtle deck of the fuselage. It could be a perilous job! (National Archives)

Radioman 3rd Class G. H. Lane grapples the hoist hook while the pilot of the Kingfisher, Ensign L. A. Williams, reaches back to hold onto Lane's belt as the floatplane is buffeted by choppy seas on 6 September 1941. This was the number-three Kingfisher assigned to VO-1. The name "*Arizona*" appears in small white letters below the black side number. (Naval History and Heritage Command)

In another photo taken on 6 September 1941, crewmen of the USS *Arizona* maneuver a Vought OS2U Kingfisher onto the fantail catapult. The sailor to the right is holding the hook used to snag the recovery sled. The launch cart, the sliding cradle/shuttle on which the center pontoon of the Kingfisher will rest, is to the right of the officer. (Naval History and Heritage Command)

The *Arizona* is moored off Ford Island at Pearl Harbor on 11 August 1941. Evidence indicates that at that time the ship was painted in Measure 1 camouflage, with Dark Gray (5-D) from the waterline to the level even with the top of the funnel, and Light Gray (5-L) above the funnel. The ship may have received a complete repainting, possibly including Sea Blue (5-S), while in drydock in November 1941. (Don Preul collection)

This photograph was taken on 8 November 1941 to document the removal of silt from Drydock 2 at Pearl Harbor, but it was perhaps the final photograph of USS *Arizona* before the 7 December attack, for the ship is visible to the upper right in Drydock 1, receiving repairs after a collision with USS *Oklahoma*. Her light-colored mast tops are visible, with the foremast being partially obscured by the drydock crane. (Don Preul collection)

USS *Arizona* (left) is moored off Ford Island at Pearl Harbor on 13 October 1941, at the same position the ship would occupy on the fatal morning of 7 December. There is a very noticeable contrast between the color of the upper portions of the masts and the control tops as opposed to the shade of gray below that level. The exact colors used on the *Arizona* on 7 December remain controversial. (Ron W. Smith collection)

Moments before 8:00 a.m. on 7 December 1941, the Japanese launched a massive aerial surprise attack on the U.S. Pacific Fleet at Pearl Harbor. USS *Arizona*, moored on Battleship Row, had already suffered at least one bomb hit when an 800kg bomb penetrated the forecastle deck around 8:10, detonating magazines and creating a massive explosion, filmed by Captain Eric Haakensen from the hospital ship USS *Solace* (AH-5). (WWII Valor in the Pacific National Monument)

"A date which will live in infamy . . ."

The morning sun rose over Pearl Harbor on Sunday, 7 December 1941, just as it had so many times before. Most of the crew of the *Arizona* were going about their usual morning routine. The ship's band, which had placed second in a "Battle of the Bands" competition, was enjoying its reward of being allowed to sleep late in the quarters in the forecastle. At the ship's stern, the color detail was preparing to hoist the American flag at the appointed 8:00 a.m. hour. Other sailors were eating breakfast, or awaiting the call to church.

Then, at 7:50 a.m., hundreds of Japanese warplanes violated the peaceful setting of Pearl Harbor and unleashed a rain of death upon the men and ships at anchor. Bombs tore open giant, seemingly indestructible steel ships, while machine gun fire ripped into the men on *Arizona's* deck. Swooping in at 10,480 feet above the harbor, a five-plane flight of horizontal bombers targeted the *Arizona*. One of the 1,756-pound (No. 80) bombs each of these aircraft carried found its mark, striking *Arizona's* number-four turret face, glancing off and exploding with minimal damage below decks. One minute later, a second flight of five like-armed bombers closed in on *Arizona*. Lieutenant Shojiro Kondo released the bomb that penetrated *Arizona's* deck near turret two. Seven seconds later, at 8:07 a.m., the tons of 14-inch powder bags held in the forward magazines erupted in a horrific explosion.

The blast ripped the forward section of the ship asunder, vaporizing steel and crew alike. *Arizona's* band was no more, nor her captain, Franklin Van Valkenberg; nor Admiral Kidd, for whom *Arizona* was his flagship; nor scores of other sailors. Debris, heavy Bunker C fuel oil, bodies, and body parts showered the decks of *Arizona,* surrounding ships, Ford Island and the surface of the harbor. In all, 1,177 U.S. servicemen died aboard *Arizona.* Many of them perished instantly when the magazines detonated, but scores of others suffered agonizing deaths in the ensuing flames, or bled to death from ghastly dismemberments.

Captain Franklin Van Valkenburg was the commanding officer of USS *Arizona* at the time of her destruction at Pearl Harbor. Born in 1888 and a 1909 graduate of the U.S. Naval Academy, he took command of the *Arizona* on 5 February 1941. At the beginning of the 7 December attack, Valkenburg directed the ship's defenses from the navigation bridge, where he died in the massive blast. The USS *Van Valkenburg* (DD-656) was named in his honor.

Rear Admiral Isaac C. Kidd Sr. was commander of Battleship Division 1 on 7 December 1941. At the commencement of the Japanese attack, he rushed to the bridge of his flagship, USS *Arizona,* where he was killed in the explosion of the forward magazines. He was posthumously awarded the Medal of Honor, which cited that he "courageously discharged his duties as Senior Officer Present Afloat" before his death.

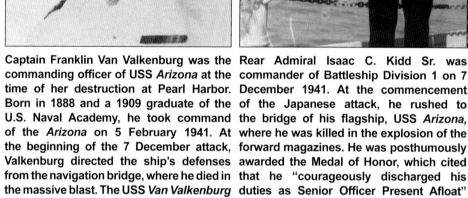

The USS *Arizona* continues to burn as boats make a sweep for survivors. The massive explosion essentially vaporized the internal forward part of the ship, causing the foremast and superstructure to tilt forward and other structures to collapse into the void. The aft part of the hull remained buoyant, although the main deck was barely above water, and the mainmast and boat/aircraft cranes were still intact. (Library of Congress)

Old Glory continues to wave from the stern of USS *Arizona* (center) as fires and smoke billow from the wreck. Nearby are other stricken ships on Battleship Row. USS *West Virginia* (BB-48) sits on the bottom of the harbor to the left, with USS *Tennessee* (BB-43) to her starboard side. The ships on Battleship Row were indeed sitting ducks to a determined, well planned Japanese attack. (National Archives)

The foremast and forward control top of USS *Arizona,* blackened by smoke and fire, tilt precariously. At the top of the control top is a platform installed between early August and mid-October 1941, intended to hold a radar antenna. Other recent modifications were the enlarged yardarms protruding from the control top, and Mk. 19 directors for the 5-inch antiaircraft guns (the box-shaped structure above the support column to the right is the port director). (National Archives)

Aft of the mainmast was a jumble of twisted, wrecked splinter shields for the guns of the secondary battery. The mainmast and control top escaped major discoloration from fire and smoke, and in this photo still displays its two-tone camouflage measure, with a lighter-colored upper section and darker gray lower section. Fifty-caliber gun barrels can be seen protruding from the birdbath gun tub atop the main control top. (National Archives)

Lieutenant Commander Samuel Glenn Fuqua (1899–1987) was the damage-control officer of USS *Arizona* on 7 December 1941. It was not his first service aboard the ship, as he had been assigned to the *Arizona* following his 1923 graduation from the U.S. Naval Academy. Although temporarily knocked unconscious when a bomb struck the stern of the ship in the opening moments of the December 7 attack, he rallied and, as senior surviving officer, directed rescue and fire-fighting operations, for which he was awarded the Congressional Medal of Honor. He subsequently served as operations officer for the Commander of the Seventh Fleet and, after World War II, as chief of staff of the Eighth Naval District. Fuqua retired from active duty as a rear admiral in 1953. He died in 1987 in Decatur, Georgia, and was laid to rest in Arlington National Cemetery in Virginia. (WWII Valor in the Pacific National Monument)

As a three-year-old child, Henry Williams Jr., the son of a naval contractor, placed the first bolt into the keel of what would become the USS *Arizona.* He grew up to be a U.S. Naval officer, serving as a lieutenant on the staff of Rear Admiral Robert A. Theobald at Pearl Harbor on 7 December 1941. On the day of the attack, Admiral Theobald, commander of Destroyer Flotilla One, dispatched Williams, acting as his staff duty officer, to retrieve war plans from a safe on the light cruiser USS *Raleigh* (CL-7), which had been torpedoed and was listing. Williams executed the task. That night, on the deck of the destroyer tender USS *Dobbin* (AD-3), he watched the battleship burn, having been present at its birth and death. He later recounted that the *Arizona* and the other battleships were burning so brightly, he was able to read a newspaper from the glare. Subsequently, as a lieutenant commander, Williams commanded the destroyer USS *Ammen* (DD-527) from 22 April 1943 to 11 May 1944. (US Naval Academy)

89

As smoke continues to billow from the *Arizona,* visible on the platform below the searchlight platform on the mainmast is the aft rangefinder. A number of sailors and Marines who were in the main control top during the attack were able to escape. To the right is turret three and its catapult. The *Arizona's* Kingfisher scout/observation floatplanes were not aboard on 7 December 1941. (National Archives)

A photographer on Ford Island snapped this view of USS *Arizona* as it continues to burn on 7 December 1941. To the right is the collapsed foremast, while to the left are the mainmast, the boat/aircraft cranes, turret three, and, faintly visible, turret four. The forms of the four 36-inch searchlights are visible on the cloverleaf platform on the mainmast. Broken-out windows are visible in the compartments of the control top. (National Archives)

During and after the 7 December 1941 attack on Pearl Harbor, any available watercraft was pressed into use to fight fires and conduct rescue operations. All available hands went to work combating fires, pulling personnel out of the waters of the harbor, rescuing trapped sailors, and searching for bodies. In a photograph dated the day following the attack, a harbor tug and a garbage lighter help fight remaining fires on the *Arizona* by spraying water on the amidships area. (National Archives)

Two days after the attack, on 9 December 1941, the fires are still burning on the wreck of USS *Arizona,* and smoke continues to emanate from the ship. The collapsed foremast and the smashed superstructure rise from the water. To the right, the three 14-inch/45-caliber guns of nearly submerged turret two are visible. To the left are the booms of the boat/aircraft cranes, snatch blocks still dangling from them. (National Archives)

Crewmen on the tugboat seen in the preceding photo spray water on the smoldering hulk. Feeding the fires were the massive amounts of fuel, lubricants, and other combustibles onboard. In one of history's more ironic twists, Lt. Henry Williams Jr., USN, who had placed the first bolt in the keel of the ship in 1914, was present at Pearl Harbor during the attack and watched the USS *Arizona* as she burned on the night of 7 December. (National Archives)

The aft portion of USS *Arizona* gradually sank until the main deck was under water, as seen in this view from the port quarter on 9 December. A life raft leans against the barbette of turret three. Compelling evidence recently surfaced that the tops of turrets one and two of USS *Arizona* were painted red at the time of the December 7 attack, as a recognition sign for Battleship Division 1, and the top of turret four was also painted red, but to denote the *Arizona* as flagship of the division. (National Archives)

USS *Widgeon* (ASR-1), a submarine-rescue ship, stands by off the stern of the *Arizona*. At sunset on 7 December, two officers of USS *Arizona*, Lt. Kleber Masterson and Ensign Leon Grabowski, had taken down the American flag from the flagstaff on the stern, but a new flag had been placed on the flagstaff by the time this photo was taken. The white awning on the fantail was in place when the attack began. (National Archives)

Boats spray water on the *Arizona* in this view from astern, probably taken several days after the 7 December attack. The awning over the fantail is visible forward of the aircraft crane. The masts of other battleships rise in the distance. To the right is Ford Island, and between the island and the wreck of the *Arizona* is a concrete mooring quay, one of two to which the *Arizona* was moored on 7 December 1941. (National Archives)

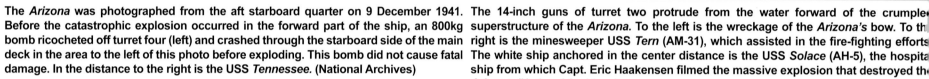

The *Arizona* was photographed from the aft starboard quarter on 9 December 1941. Before the catastrophic explosion occurred in the forward part of the ship, an 800kg bomb ricocheted off turret four (left) and crashed through the starboard side of the main deck in the area to the left of this photo before exploding. This bomb did not cause fatal damage. In the distance to the right is the USS *Tennessee*. (National Archives)

The wreckage of the *Arizona's* superstructure, mainmast, and main control top were photographed from off the port bow on 10 December 1941. The massive explosion of the forward magazines caused these structures to collapse. Above and aft of turret two is the conning tower, with its vision slits apparent. On the rangefinder platform above the conning tower are the 20' rangefinder and the port Mk. 19 director. (National Archives, San Francisco, via Tracy White)

The 14-inch guns of turret two protrude from the water forward of the crumpled superstructure of the *Arizona*. To the left is the wreckage of the *Arizona's* bow. To the right is the minesweeper USS *Tern* (AM-31), which assisted in the fire-fighting efforts. The white ship anchored in the center distance is the USS *Solace* (AH-5), the hospital ship from which Capt. Eric Haakensen filmed the massive explosion that destroyed the *Arizona*. (National Archives)

The fires aboard USS *Arizona* had been extinguished for several days when this photo was taken on 12 December 1941. Seemingly defying gravity, the foremast continues to teeter forward. The splinter shields, installed a year earlier to give antiaircraft gun crews some protection, are now a twisted, warped mass. Below them, several 5-inch/51-caliber guns protrude from casemates. (National Archives, San Francisco, via Tracy White)

The formal salvage operation at Pearl Harbor began one week after the attack, on 14 December, thirteen days before this photograph of the wreckage was taken. Motor launches are positioned alongside the wreck as crews begin to assess the prospects of salvaging parts of the ship. USS *Tennessee* is not present in the background, having been returned service a week earlier. (Naval History and Heritage Command)

The call to avenge the sneak attack on Pearl Harbor became an important rallying cry in America's drive to defeat Japan. This wartime poster featuring the likeness of a sailor brandishing a clenched fist also includes a view of the destruction of USS *Arizona*. The publication of photographs of the twisted, bent wreckage of the ship's foremast and superstructure gave the public an iconic image of the ship's destruction.

Although this poster dating from the United States's early months of involvement in World War II portrays an inaccurate vision of the attack on Pearl Harbor, it makes up in spirit and composition what it lacks in accuracy. Behind the fist-waving, hatless Uncle Sam is a severely listing battleship, complete with tripod masts with control tops reminiscent of the USS *Arizona*.

Salvage

Arizona burned until Tuesday, 9 December, and almost as soon as the fire was out she was boarded by an inspection party, who landed on the boat deck, the only deck still above water. Incredibly, however, some of the ship's company had boarded her on the 8th and recovered valuable papers and cash, which they duly turned over to salvage authorities. Shortly thereafter, work began recovering bodies from the part of the ship that stood above the waters of Pearl Harbor. Early on it was determined that *Arizona* was a total loss, and on 22 December work began stripping the ship of items that would be of use to the fleet – or to Hawaii's defense.

Navy salvage divers removed needed ammunition for reconditioning, along with *Arizona's* smaller weapons. Responding to mounting pressure from bereaved families, the Navy ordered salvage divers to recover bodies for burial. This effort proved futile, as in the months after the attack, sea life and decomposition had rendered *Arizona's* remaining crew aboard too unstable for recovery or identification. Accordingly, the decision was reached to leave them entombed aboard their ship. The mechanics of the ship were another matter – after the usable and repairable equipment topsides had been removed, the remaining superstructure above water was removed as scrap steel. Eventually, salvage teams removed *Arizona's* after main battery turrets entirely, and the guns from turret two. The latter were ultimately installed as replacements for worn barrels on USS *Nevada,* while the former were first mounted as coastal defense batteries protecting Oahu, and then, after World War II, were unceremoniously scrapped.

To help the war effort, movie director John Ford put together a film unit for what would become the Office of Strategic Services (OSS). In late March 1942 the unit filmed the devastation at Pearl Harbor in preparation for a feature-length film, *December 7th.* **One still from that film is this 16mm Kodachrome shot of the starboard side of *Arizona*'s mainmast, showing that the searchlights and directors had already been salvaged. (Naval History and Heritage Command)**

With the U.S. flag still waving adjacent to the searchlight platform, USS *Arizona's* mainmast is viewed from the starboard quarter sometime between 22 December 1941, when her searchlights were salvaged, and 22 July 1942, by which time the portside crane had been removed. The sailors are standing on the platform that formerly held the 12-foot rangefinder. (National Archives)

In a photograph taken 17 February 1942, the forward superstructure of the *Arizona* is shown in the collapsed condition it suffered from the massive explosion of the forward part of the ship on 7 December 1941. On the platform to the right is the forward rangefinder. (Naval History and Heritage Command)

In another photograph taken on 17 February 1942, one of the 5-inch/51-caliber casemate guns in the superstructure points outward. Splinter shields for five-inch antiaircraft guns that already had been salvaged are along the twisted edge of the deck. (WWII Valor in the Pacific National Monument)

Viewed from the port side of USS *Arizona* facing aft on 17 February 1942, the wreckage of the forward superstructure is to the far left, while toward the right is the mainmast, on each side of which are the boat cranes, with blocks and cables still rigged to them. (Library of Congress)

On 22 July 1942 a temporary wharf connects mooring quay F7 with the remains of USS *Arizona*. Although the mainmast had not escaped the 7 December attack completely unscathed, it still stood defiantly seven months later. Next to the mainmast is the starboard crane. (National Archives)

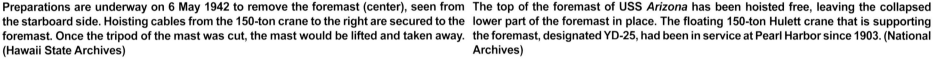

Preparations are underway on 6 May 1942 to remove the foremast (center), seen from the starboard side. Hoisting cables from the 150-ton crane to the right are secured to the foremast. Once the tripod of the mast was cut, the mast would be lifted and taken away. (Hawaii State Archives)

The top of the foremast of USS *Arizona* has been hoisted free, leaving the collapsed lower part of the foremast in place. The floating 150-ton Hulett crane that is supporting the foremast, designated YD-25, had been in service at Pearl Harbor since 1903. (National Archives)

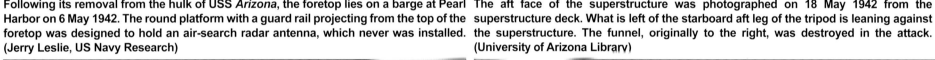

Following its removal from the hulk of USS *Arizona*, the foretop lies on a barge at Pearl Harbor on 6 May 1942. The round platform with a guard rail projecting from the top of the foretop was designed to hold an air-search radar antenna, which never was installed. (Jerry Leslie, US Navy Research)

The aft face of the superstructure was photographed on 18 May 1942 from the superstructure deck. What is left of the starboard aft leg of the tripod is leaning against the superstructure. The funnel, originally to the right, was destroyed in the attack. (University of Arizona Library)

The boat deck (or, the aft part of the superstructure deck) is viewed from the mainmast looking forward, with the circular opening for the funnel, which had been removed, to the center. To the right and the left are the boat cranes, and at the top is a leg of the foremast. (WWII Valor in the Pacific National Monument)

By 27 May 1942, salvage teams were well on their way to completely cutting away Arizona's forward superstructure. (Jerry Leslie, U.S. Navy Research)

This view taken from the mainmast shows the same area portrayed in the preceding photo, on the same date. Most of the foremast had been removed two weeks earlier. The guns of turret two and the round platform for the 20-foot rangefinder are at the top. (Library of Congress)

This 19 July 1942 view from the bow documents items to be removed, including wreckage of the bow (foreground), the starboard crane, and the mainmast. Above the temporary pier is the conning tower, and below the pier are turret two's gun muzzles. (National Archives)

The wreckage of USS *Arizona* is viewed from aft on 19 July 1942. The aircraft crane protrudes from the water in the foreground. Between the crane and the mainmast are the remains of turrets three and four, traversed to starboard and their guns removed. (National Archives)

Although the flag bridge aft of the conning tower had been removed, the conning tower rises to the left, with a splinter shield partially surrounding it. Vision slits are apparent in the tower, which was formed of armor 16 inches thick on the sides and 8 inches on top. (National Archives)

On 30 September 1942, an "unwatering" operation is underway to pump water out of the aft ammunition magazines. Turret three, now pointing to the starboard and her guns removed, is to the left of center. To the right, the superstructure has now been removed. (Naval History and Heritage Command)

By 26 January 1943, when this aerial photograph was taken, much of the wreckage had been removed from the hulk of USS *Arizona*. To the lower right are turrets three and four. The light colored structures between the hulk and Ford Island were concrete mooring quays. (National Archives)

Two barnacle-clad 5-inch/51-caliber guns of USS *Arizona*'s secondary battery rest on a pier at Pearl Harbor after being salvaged from the ship. These were also referred to as broadside guns. On the side of each mount is the pointer's handwheel and the elevating worm wheel. (Naval History and Heritage Command)

During the USS *Arizona* salvage operation, extensive use was made of divers, like this party photographed in May 1943, who worked within the sunken ship to retrieve corpses, documents, and other valuable items, and outside the ship, to survey the damage, remove hazards, and stabilize the hulk. (Naval History and Heritage Command)

Turrets three (foreground) and four, photographed from above on 18 May 1942, had been rotated to the starboard side, and all that was left standing were their sides. On the wooden beams atop turret three is a deep-well pump, with discharged water spewing out of the duct to the lower right. (Naval History and Heritage Command)

By 17 July 1942, air ventilation ducts had been installed in turret three (foreground), in addition to the water-pumping apparatus. Fresh air was essential to the salvage crews working in the noxious atmosphere within the ship. At the forward end of the gun house (left) are salvaged powder canisters. (Naval History and Heritage Command)

A pump is discharging water from magazines below decks on platform two, into a flexible boom (left), to contain any oil discharge. A wooden catwalk and steps had been installed around the gun house of turret four. The photo was taken on 5 October 1942. (Naval History and Heritage Command)

Workmen removing ammunition from the *Arizona's* first-platform magazines take a brief rest on 1 July 1942. The man at the left with the respirator was on the topside work crew, while the men in the protective suits and oxygen masks worked down in the magazines. (Naval History and Heritage Command)

Salvage workers use this winch, seen mounted on the floor of turret three on 29 June 1942, to hoist ammunition up and out of the magazines. Salvaged powder canisters, also called tanks, are arrayed on the floor of the turret. (Naval History and Heritage Command)

These men, photographed on 5 October 1942, were part of the crew removing ammunition through turret three. Poisonous gases, principally hydrogen sulfide, would build up in the unwatered compartments, necessitating the use of respirators and oxygen masks. (Naval History and Heritage Command)

Toxic gasses were not the only hazard confronting workmen in the hulk of the *Arizona*. Water is seen here cascading into one of turret four's ammunition handling rooms during salvage operations in early October 1942. Leaks in a water shed on the main deck were the source of the deluge. (Naval History and Heritage Command)

Turret three was photographed from its aft quarter on 29 June 1942. The rear and the front of the gun house had been removed, allowing a view inside. On the floor is a small winch. A Caterpillar Diesel-powered pump and water-discharge pipe are atop the gun house. (Naval History and Heritage Command)

Two men help hoist ammunition from the magazines of the *Arizona* on 1 July 1942 while another man at the top left watches the procedure. Removed ammunition would later be sent to an ammunition depot for reconditioning. (Naval History and Heritage Command)

Inside the remains of the gun house of turret three on 1 July 1942, workers wearing respirators hoist 14-inch powder canisters from the magazines. Powering the hoist was the small, compressed-air-powered winch in the background, called a tugger. (Naval History and Heritage Command)

Following its removal from its mounting on the ship, the gun house of turret three is hoisted into place prior to being shipped to a storage facility onshore. Much of the lifting of *Arizona's* heavy turret components was performed by YD-25, the 150-ton floating crane. (WWII Valor in the Pacific National Monument)

The gun house of turret three has been removed from the hulk of USS *Arizona* on 19 April 1943, while above and behind it, a crane is lifting the rotating structure of the turret that had been positioned below the gun house, inside the barbette of turret three. (WWII Valor in the Pacific National Monument)

The gun house of turret three is hoisted from the barbette on 19 April 1943. The official salvage diary states that this work was delayed by one day because of problems in bringing the 150-ton floating crane into position alongside the ship. (Hawaii State Archives)

The gun house of turret three has just been removed from the USS *Arizona*, exposing the interior of the upper part of the barbette to view, on 19 April 1942. Rollers upon which the turret rotated are positioned on top of the foundation of the turret, within the barbette. (WWII Valor in the Pacific National Monument)

The lowest components of the rotating part of turret three have been hoisted from the barbette on 25 April 1943. On that date, the remaining parts of that turret, including the foundation ring and rollers, hold-down clips, and lower parts of the powder hoists, were removed. (Hawaii State Archives)

This view, dated 25 April 1943, shows the inside of barbette three after the foundation of the turret had been removed. Below the framework in the foreground, support beams are visible. At the bottom of the barbette is a jumble of debris and oily water. (WWII Valor in the Pacific National Monument)

The foundation of turret three is hoisted from the barbette, the top of which is visible at the bottom of this photo dated 25 April 1943. Faintly visible at the top of the assembly are the tops of the rollers upon which the turret rotated, as well as their axle retainers. (WWII Valor in the Pacific National Monument)

In a photo dated 3 May 1943, a section of armor plate has been hoisted free of the aft starboard side of the gun house in the water below it. The oblong cutout at the top of the section accommodated the optical rangefinder. Ford Island is in the background. (Hawaii State Archives)

On 11 December 1942, one year and four days after the destruction of USS *Arizona*, part of the roof of turret two's gun house has been removed for access, exposing the oil- and water-filled interior. In the background is a floating wharf mounted on pontoons. (Hawaii State Archives)

Looking inside the opening on the roof of gun house two as pumps work to remove water in April 1943, the breeches of two 14-inch/45-caliber guns are visible, coated with oil and mud. The three guns of that turret were removed, but the sides of the gun house were left in place. (Hawaii State Archives)

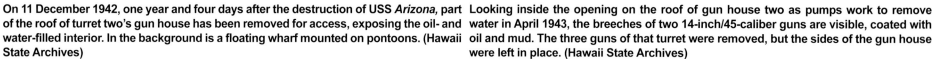

The center 14-inch/45-caliber gun has been hoisted from turret two of USS *Arizona* during the salvage operation in early August 1943. A 150-ton crane was used in this operation, and two divers were employed in making underwater rigging connections. (Hawaii State Archives)

With the pumping of water from turret two complete, in mid-September 1943 the front of the gun house is removed, and a 150-ton crane hoisted free the slides for the 14-inch guns. The starboard side of the slide and face plate assembly is in view, with the trunnion to the right. (Hawaii State Archives)

The slides from turret two are suspended from the 150-ton crane after being removed from the gun house, with the rears of the slides in view. By then, the 14-inch/45-caliber Mk. 8 Mod. 4 guns had been removed from turrets three and four and would soon see new use – on land. (Hawaii State Archives)

Two men at Pearl Harbor Navy Yard do preservation work on the slide of one of the turrets of USS *Arizona*. The front of the slide is in view, with its left trunnion appearing at the far right of the photograph. In the background, lying on its side, is a cage mast salvaged from one of the battleships at Pearl Harbor, showing the intricately criss-crossed pipes that made up the structure. (National Archives)

After the removal of the 14-inch guns from turrets two through four, the weapons were transported to the Pearl Harbor Navy Yard and placed in a state of preservation, for possible future use. Here, members of a work crew apply grease with their bare hands to a 14-inch gun. To the left, the breech block is removed, exposing the interrupted threads of the breech to view. (National Archives)

A salvage crewman works on one USS *Arizona's* two catapults. Both catapults had been removed and stored at Waipio Point by early May 1942. The Type P Mk. IV Mod. 1 catapult on turret three suffered heat damage but was considered salvageable, and the Type P Mk. VI catapult had shrapnel damage but was repaired. (National Archives)

After turrets three and four and their guns were removed from the hulk, they were transferred to the U.S. Army. Plans were developed to emplace the turrets in two defensive positions on the Oahu coast: Battery *Arizona*, at Kahe Point, and Battery *Pennsylvania,* at Mokapu Point. Shown here is Battery *Pennsylvania* on 22 March 1945, with the gun house to the right. To the left, workmen are preparing to hoist the slide and faceplate assembly of the turret, using the massive crane in the background. (National Archives)

Workmen are seen from another angle as they attach a hoist to the very heavy slide assembly at Battery *Pennsylvania* on 22 March 1945. The port trunnion of the slide is in view. The slide supported all three of the 14-inch/45-caliber guns of the turret, and it was by means of the slide that all three guns elevated in unison. After the slide was installed in the gun house of Battery *Pennsylvania,* the front and the top plates of the turret would be set in place. (US Army Museum of Hawaii)

Lying below the surface at Batteries *Arizona* and *Pennsylvania,* dug at great labor and expense into the rock, were networks of chambers for ammunition storage, generators, and radar, radio, and plotting rooms. Shown here is the shell storage room of Battery *Pennsylvania* on 22 March 1945, being used to store electrical wire and supplies. There is a chain hoist at the end of each of the two I-beams running from front to rear in the photo. (US Army Museum of Hawaii)

The powder room at Battery *Pennsylvania,* seen here, probably was similar to the powder room at Battery *Arizona,* which was 108 feet long, 20 feet wide, and 15 feet high. The room was equipped with three 125-kilowatt diesel-powered generators, with an exhaust system and huge (at least 10,000-gallon) fuel tanks below the floor. The room also contained such equipment as an electrical fuse panel, air compressors, and water coolers. (US Army Museum of Hawaii)

Battery *Arizona,* shown with her 14-inch/45-caliber guns installed in the gun house, was almost completed when World War II ended. With the end of the war and the threat of enemy invasion diminished, work ceased on the two batteries centered around USS *Arizona's* salvaged main-battery turrets, and the batteries were abandoned. (US Army Museum of Hawaii)

With covers fitted over the muzzles, the 14-inch/45-caliber guns of Battery *Arizona* overlook the coast of Oahu. Just as these guns, when installed on the USS *Arizona,* were never fired in anger, they would not be fired in combat from their positions at Battery *Arizona* and Battery *Pennsylvania,* although the latter's guns were test-fired in August 1945. (US Army Museum of Hawaii)

1945-1950

In the days immediately following the 7 December attack, just under 200 bodies of her crew were removed from the above-water portion of the ship, or plucked from the waters of Pearl Harbor. The 1942 attempt to recover further remains yielded 105 more *Arizona* crewmen, the rest of the crew remaining in their ship. Salvage efforts, documented earlier in this book, removed tons of material from the ship, some reusable, some merely scrap to be smelted and forged into new war materiel.

After the 1943 salvage activity, *Arizona's* hulk lay largely undisturbed, both a somber reminder of the U.S. Navy's lowest ebb, and also an impediment to the Navy's use of Pearl Harbor, not only to Berth F-7, where she sank, but also to adjacent berths, which now required careful maneuvering to use. Consideration had been given during the war to raising a portion of the wreck, and demolishing the remainder by blasting, or even using the hulk to test the effectiveness of shaped charges.

By 1947 the decision had been made to leave *Arizona* in place – a tomb for her perished crew. Periodic surveys were made during the late 1940s, but no changes were made to the vessel until Admiral Arthur Radford, Commander in Chief, Pacific Command, ordered that a flagpole be affixed to the hulk, and a small wooden platform be installed on the ship. By his order, the flag was to raised daily on the *Arizona,* although *Arizona* has not been a commissioned U.S. warship since stricken from the Navy Vessel Register on 1 December 1942. This tradition continues to this day.

On 19 March 1948, officers look over the remnants of the superstructure deck amidships on USS *Arizona*. Before the destruction of the ship, this part of the deck was the area where boats were stored on cradles. Below the deck were the central galley and potato and vegetable lockers. (National Archives)

The site of the break of the deck is viewed from aft, facing toward Ford Island, in a photo probably taken in the late 1940s. The main deck is submerged to the left, while remnants of the galley and boat deck are from the center to the left. The vertical cylinder toward the right is the lower part of the aft leg of the mainmast. (National Archives)

In 1950 a flagpole was attached to the remnants of the aft leg of the mainmast, and the U.S. flag was raised and lowered every day. In the foreground are vents, while the bottom of the aft leg of the mainmast is adjacent to the flag staff. The effects of corrosion from years of exposure to the harbor's water are evident. (Getty Images)

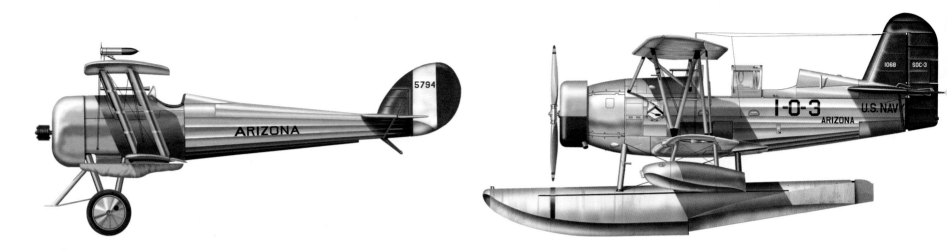

The first aircraft launched from *Arizona* were Nieuport 28 land planes, taking off from flying platforms mounted atop turret two, and supported by the 14-inch rifles. The aircraft was hastily repainted, with its drab original finish sometimes bleeding through its new silver color.

This SOC-3 Bureau Number 1084 was assigned to the USS *Arizona* in 1938, as indicated by the red on its cowl, matching the roof of *Arizona's* turret four. Its red tail is indicative of its belonging to Squadron VO-1, assigned to Battleship Division One, matching the roofs of turrets one and two.

After its modernization in 1929-1931, but prior to July 1941, USS *Arizona* wore the typical #5 Standard Navy Gray paint scheme, as seen here. In July 1941 she was repainted into the camouflage Measure 1 scheme shown on the cover of this book.

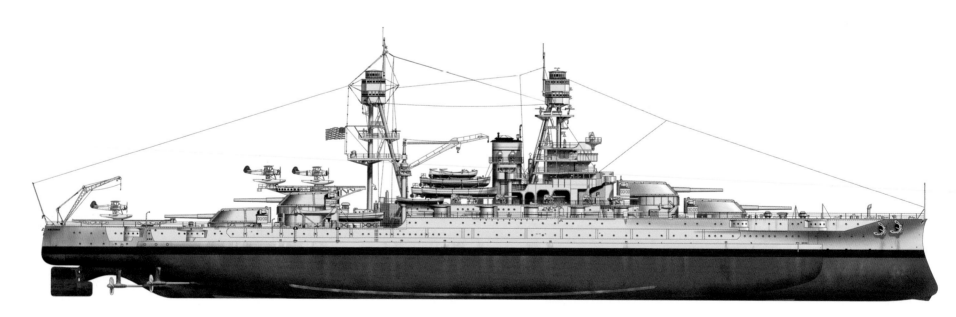

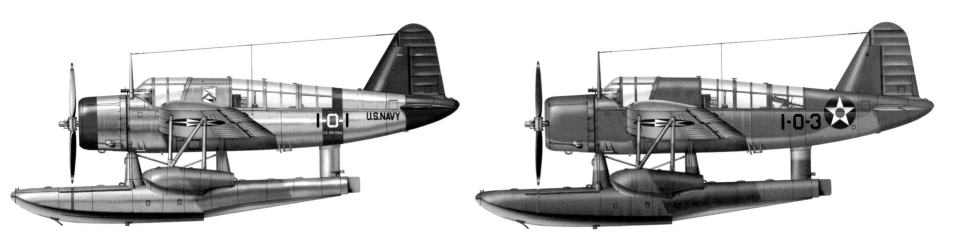

Vought OS2U-1 Kingfishers replaced the Curtiss SOC-3 Seagulls, but continued the paint scheme of their predecessors. This aircraft, Bureau Number 1695, which carries the red fuselage band of the Section Leader, also had red chevrons on wing tops.

When *Arizona's* Kingfishers were upgraded to the OS2U-3 model, at the same time the colorful prewar paint scheme gave way to the blue and gray camouflage scheme shown here. These were the aircraft assigned at the time the ship was lost.

Many scholars believe that at the time of the Pearl Harbor attack *Arizona* was to have been painted a modified camouflaged Measure 1 scheme with 5-S Sea Blue, replacing the normal 5-D Dark Gray. Evidence, however, is inconclusive as to whether this repainting was fully implemented before the fateful day.

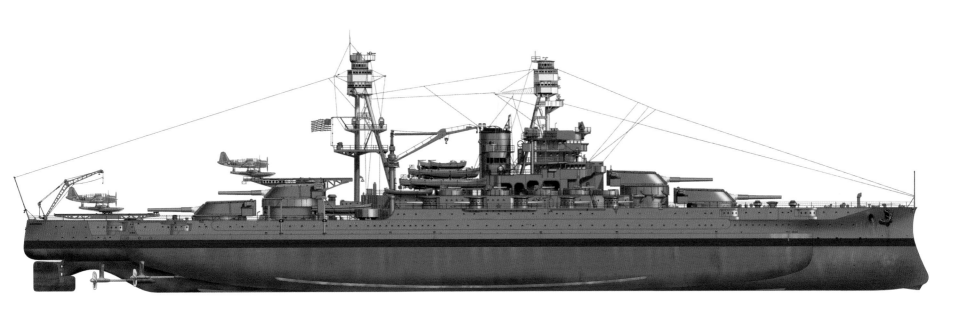

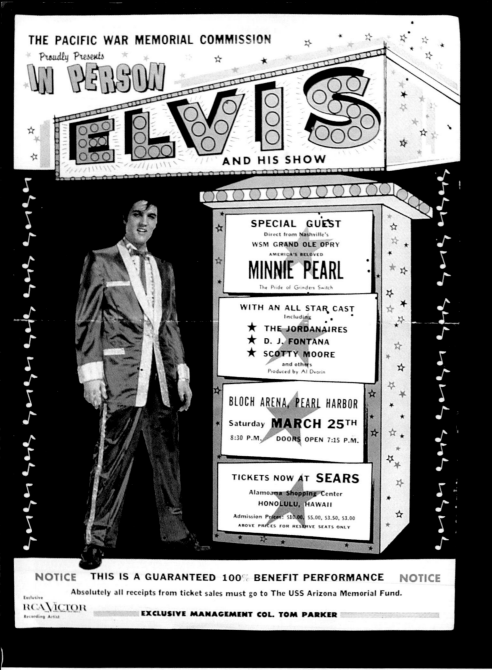

In the late 1950s, Congress authorized the construction of a memorial to USS *Arizona*. To raise funds for this memorial, Elvis Presley staged a benefit concert on 25 March 1961 at Pearl Harbor's Bloch Arena. The sold-out concert, a poster for which is shown here, reportedly raised almost $65,000 for the memorial. (WWII Valor in the Pacific National Monument)

Arizona Memorial

Discussions concerning a memorial to the servicemen lost at Pearl Harbor began in 1943, even as the war wore on. Despite various proposals, but for Admiral Radford's mounting of a flag pole on *Arizona's* wreck in 1950, nothing of substance came until 7 December 1955, when a 10-foot, 27-ton stone with a bronze plaque mounted was placed on Ford Island, near *Arizona's* resting place. H. Tucker Gratz, Navy veteran and Hawaii businessman, had been lobbying for a memorial since 1946, and while involved in the 1955 monument, believed that something more substantial would be a more appropriate memorial to the 1,177 men lost on *Arizona,* and the thousands more lost from Pearl Harbor and throughout the Pacific.

The campaign by Gratz and others began to pay off on 15 March 1958, when President Dwight Eisenhower signed into law a bill authorizing the construction of the USS *Arizona* Memorial – without the use of Federal funds. The project was given an initial push by a contribution from the Territory of Hawaii in the amount of $50,000. This was followed quickly by $95,000 raised following Medal of Honor winner and *Arizona* survivor Samuel Fuqua's appearance on *This is Your Life.* Fundraising then largely stagnated until a 1961 benefit concert in Hawaii by Elvis Presley, which raised $64,000 and renewed interest in the project. A further $40,000 was raised through an arrangement with Revell, Inc., then the world's largest maker of plastic model kits. Ultimately, Federal dollars were required to bring the project to completion. These were secured by decorated veteran and Hawaii Senator Daniel Inouye. Architect Alfred Preis's striking design, which does not touch *Arizona* herself, is said to represent the low point of nation, rising in the end. Preis is one of two non-crew members now interred within Arizona.

"The King" accepts an Award of Honor from the Pacific War Memorial Commission for his efforts in raising funds for the USS *Arizona* Memorial. This presentation was staged at the Hilton Hawaiian Village Hotel, Honolulu, on the day of the concert. To the right is Presley's manager, Colonel Tom Parker. (WWII Valor in the Pacific National Monument)

Construction of the USS *Arizona* Memorial commenced in late 1960. Hawaiian architect Alfred Preis designed the memorial. Here, the memorial is taking shape, with a platform spanning the amidships section of the ship resting on piers on either side of the ship. The memorial was designed to accommodate 200 people. (WWII Valor in the Pacific National Monument)

Work progresses on the USS *Arizona* Memorial in the early 1960s. The view is from the harbor side of the structure facing toward Ford Island. To the right, several remaining ship's ventilators are visible, to the right of which is the barbette of turret three, on top of which a temporary platform has been placed to hold construction equipment. (WWII Valor in the Pacific National Monument)

The USS *Arizona* Memorial nears completion on 30 March 1962. A covered enclosure with a curved roof had been built on the platform spanning the hulk of the ship. The curved roof was symbolic of America's prewar prowess, the dip in morale occasioned by the Pearl Harbor attack, and subsequent restoration of national pride. (WWII Valor in the Pacific National Monument)

The memorial is viewed from close-up during the final stages of construction. Large windows on the sides of the memorial would allow visitors to view the remains of the ship below the water, as well as observe the harbor. These seven windows on each side of the structure and on the roof commemorate the date of the attack, 7 December. (WWII Valor in the Pacific National Monument)

Sailors and a civilian tourist stand on the ramp from the boat landing in this twilight view. The flag pole is still attached to the lower part of the aft leg of the mainmast. In the background to the right is the USS *Arizona* mooring quay, one of two concrete quays to which the ship was moored on the morning of 7 December 1941. (Department of Defense)

On 7 December 1941, 1,177 men lost their lives on the USS *Arizona,* and most of them remain entombed there. The remains of USS *Arizona* are a U.S. military cemetery. This tablet on the USS *Arizona* Memorial commemorates the names of the members of the U.S. Navy and U.S. Marine Corps who perished on the ship on 7 December. (WWII Valor in the Pacific National Monument)

The ashes of some of the 334 crewmen of the USS *Arizona* who survived the 7 December attack have been interred in the well of barbette four in the remains of the ship. A marble marker inside the USS *Arizona* Memorial lists those crewmen and their years of death. Visitors place leis in front of the names of the fallen as a gesture of respect and remembrance. (Department of Defense)

Illuminated at night, the USS *Arizona* Memorial seems to float over the remains of the ship and the more than one thousand men who died on her. Dedicated on 30 May 1962, Memorial Day, the memorial is visited by over one million people annually, and it now is part of the World War II Valor in the Pacific National Monument. (Department of Defense)